How to get a *Blackbelt* in Writing

By Aiki Flinthart
2020

To all the authors out there – both published and aspiring – don't listen to the self-doubt and don't give up. You are good enough.

Thank you to my wonderful, supportive husband, who never complained about the amount of time I spent doing martial arts, or writing, or all the other crazy things I've tried. In fact, many of them we did together. He is absolutely the best.

How to get a Blackbelt in Writing

Cover artwork by Pamela Jeffs
Copyright © 2020 Aiki Flinthart
All rights reserved. No part of this publication may be reproduced, stored in a retrieval system, or transmitted in any form or by any means, by any person or entity (including Google, Amazon or similar organisations) without the prior permission in writing of the copyright holder concerned, nor be otherwise circulated in any form of binding or cover other than that in which it is published and without a similar condition, including this condition, being imposed on the subsequent purchaser.

A Cataloging-in-Publications entry for this title is available from the National Library of Australia.

ISBN-13: 978-0-6487736-9-6 (Trade Paperback)
ISBN-13: 978-0-6487736-8-9 (e-book)
CAT Press
PO Box 3388, Darra
QLD 4076, Australia

Discover other titles by Aiki Flinthart at:
www.aikiflinthart.com

Including:

The 80AD series (YA Adventure/Fantasy)
80AD Book 1: *The Jewel of Asgard*
80AD Book 2: *The Hammer of Thor*
80AD Book 3: *The Tekhen of Anuket*
80AD Book 4: *The Sudarshana*
80AD Book 5: *The Yu Dragon*

The Kalima Chronicles (YA Adventure/Fantasy)
IRON – Book 1
FIRE – Book 2
STEEL – Book 3
A Future, Forged (Prequel)

Ruadhan Sidhe Novels (Urban Fantasy)
Shadows Wake – Book 1
Shadows Bane – Book 2
Shadows Fate – Book 3
Healing Heather – Book 4 (Romance)

Sold! (Contemporary Romance/Adventure)

Short Story Anthologies/Collections
Worlds in Words
The Zookeeper's Tales of Interstellar Oddities
Return
Elemental
Rogues' Gallery

NOTE:
This book is written with
AUSTRALIAN SPELLING/ENGLISH,
not USA spelling.
Don't panic.

How to get a *Blackbelt* in Writing

Aiki Flinthart 2020

Contents

Introduction 13
Part 1—Thinking Strategically 19
Part 2—Finding Your Style. 25
Part 3—Co-operation/Collaboration 31
Part 4—Warrior spirit...................................37
Part 5—Adaptability.....................................45
Part 6—Big things and Small 51
Part 7—Self-Discipline 57
Part 8—Proving Yourself.............................63
Part 9—Fear & self doubt............................69
Part 10—Commitment..................................75
Part 11—Body Awareness...........................81
Part 12—Old Techniques and New; Good and Bad 87
Part 13—Understanding People...................93
Part 14—Awareness 97
Part 15—Perseverance...............................103
Part 16—Monkey Mind / No Mind.............109
Part 17—Speed, Distance, and Timing 115
Part 18—Power 121
Part 19—Breath Control.............................127
Part 20—Self Control. 131
Part 21—Never be the Best 137
Part 22—Simplifying 141

Part 23—Prioritising 147
Part 24—Passing on Knowledge 151
Part 25—Facing Darkness—Mental Health . 159
Part 26—Writing THE END—Facing Death 167
About the Author: Aiki Flinthart 173
Discover other titles by Aiki Flinthart 178

Introduction

This little book is not about how to be a good martial artist. Hopefully it will help you hone your craft, and clarify what you want from your life and from this crazy business of being an author.

Because *How to Get a Blackbelt in Writing* is about taking life-lessons from one passion and applying them to another—and to your life as a whole. Thoughts derived from 20 years of martial arts training are transferred to life and to writing. (Insert "pen mightier than sword" joke here).

Seriously…Strange as it may sound, there are certain mindsets and skills garnered from martial arts that are astonishingly helpful in many other aspects of your world.

That's what this collection attempts to convey.

Of course, the path to good writing isn't quite like training in a dojo. You can regularly attend a good dojo and learn from a wise sensei who knows what you lack and can introduce new skills when you're ready.

It's all laid out for you, step by step.

When writing, you often feel (and are) alone, unaware of a whole bunch of craft techniques, not sure what to do next or who to listen to.

So, in addition to taking life-lessons from martial arts attitudes, this book contains a few other hints. Each module offers a thought to consider, and suggestions of steps to take or concepts to research that might help smooth the path to your writing goals.

As the book progresses, the modules drill down from the more general, to more detailed suggestions—beginning with broad concepts around publishing and business, through to specifics on writing techniques.

Because the more you learn and practice, the stronger your stories will become and the more impact they will have on a reader.

And the happier you are with your skills, the more confident you'll be with your ability to produce a good novel or short story.

Enjoying your chosen passion is important to success, no matter how you define that term.

NOTE: I don't claim to be a world expert on writing. In fact, I feel somewhat uncomfortable even creating this little How To. But I'm also aware how tough it can be to learn some of these skills on your own.

If passing on my hard-earned knowledge can help another frustrated author, I'm glad to do it. Just keep in mind that this is not comprehensive, and it's somewhat subjective. Feel free to dig further and learn more. I truly hope you do.

How am I qualified to help, you ask? Excellent question. Always ask that whenever someone claims to be an expert. (I don't believe I know everything. Anyone who says they do is lying. I'm sure I've missed things. Quite sure.)

However, I do have a few blackbelts and quite a few books under my belt (pun intended). Plus a decent number of years lived, a lot of experience in some very random things—from geology, waterskiing, scuba diving, and whitewater rafting, to skydiving, lute-playing, bellydancing, painting, archery, and knifethrowing—and a highly supportive and loving husband.

Here's a bit of background, if you're interested.

Martial Arts:

In my early 20s I started shopping around for a martial art to do. I tried several: silat, judo, karate, taekwando. Finding a suitable martial art is a personal thing. It's not just about the art, it's also about the instructor and the other students; the attitude of the dojo as a whole. Luckily, I chanced across a small Yoshinkan Aikido dojo with a dedicated, intelligent sensei.

Yoshinkan Aikido is considered a "hard" style. While brutally effective, it teaches fluidity and power over force and strength. Sometimes being strong is a disadvantage. Although Aikido has pros and cons—as do all arts—the sensei, students, and the art all suited me. I stuck with it for 20 years, although I have dabbled in other arts to fill in the curriculum gaps.

Writing:

When I started writing, I couldn't find a convenient list of what I needed to learn. So, I spent 7 years researching and created one for myself; worked my way through, finding the best courses, workshops, books, and teachers I could afford.

For the last 4 years I've been giving workshops and mentoring other authors, editing stories for them, helping with story development, and (of course) writing my own works. People seem to like what I produce, which is nice. I like my words, too, which is even better.

Who is this book for?

Anyone who either writes or wants to write—no matter what their level of skill.

Experienced authors should find some useful thoughts sequestered in amongst the Martial Arts and Writing comparisons, even if they already know the suggestions at the end of each module.

New and intermediate authors, adrift in the world of publishing, will (hopefully) find the whole book handy—especially if they're already aware there are gaps in their skillset.

No-one knows everything. Like martial artists, authors need more than our own eyes and mind to achieve writing goals. But learning to write well can be hit and miss—and very expensive if you go down the wrong path. There are a lot of scam artists out there waiting to take advantage of new writers.

Of course, there are many reputable teachers as well.

But where do you start? Who do you go to? What questions do you even ask when you don't know the publishing industry's lexicon? What crucial information do you need to know to help your writing level up?

And how, exactly, is martial arts related to writing? I mean, really, it sounds crazy, doesn't it?

Keep reading. You'll be surprised.

There should be enough pointers here to help you take your first—or next—career steps.

Plus, enough to make you stop and think about your life, your writing, and what you want from both.

Part 1—Thinking Strategically

Something to Ponder: What do you want from your writing? Do you want a multi-book writing career, or is it just a hobby you love? (There are no "right" answers, by the way. Write for your own reasons, not to please anyone else.)

These are simply helpful questions to ask yourself early on. The answers will affect what you write, how well you wrangle the words, who you write for, who you learn from, how many books/stories you write, how much marketing you do, and a host of other career-choice decisions.

Knowing the answers now can save you a lot of wandering down the wrong paths, angsting, and creating the wrong book for the wrong audience.

Martial Arts:

If you ever get a chance, read *The Art of War*, by Sun Tzu. It's a book on ancient warfare strategies, but has been read and interpreted over and over by various other industries because thinking strategically applies to any situation, and any career. It just involves the ability to look ahead and mentally play out the possibilities. Then to decide on the path that will take you to your goal.

In martial arts, you need to think ahead to achieve your goals. For most good martial artists, that goal is "avoid getting into trouble". (Aikido calls this "*avoid the falling rock*"). It starts with not going places that will put you into violent situations. Excellent strategy.

If locations are unavoidable, the next step is to think ahead when first entering a building or new situation. To assess the room, other people, look for exits, weapons, potential threats. To plan for how get out with the minimum of fuss. To be clear in your goal to protect yourself and others in the event you can't get out safely.

If conflict is unavoidable, you need to know ahead of time what result you want from the situation. What (or who) is most important to you?

When everything goes pearshaped, there's no time for planning. You must already know how to use the space, deal with multiple attackers, avoid being trapped, use tools and obstacles to your advantage.

Aikido advises you to keep moving, keep changing, keep adapting. Because if you stay still, you'll get overrun and clobbered.

Training your mind to think strategically ahead of time will help you think clearly when under stress—both of which are just as important as training your body to deal with attacks.

Writing:

Whether traditionally published or self-published, an author needs to think ahead. Decide what they want their future to look like, then plan accordingly.

Do you write to earn buckets of money and recognition? Then be prepared to be *very* strategic about how many books to write, how often to release them, your branding, marketing, and multiple streams of income.

Are you just writing for the fun of it? You'll still need to master a few basic strategies to reach even a small audience of loyal readers.

Creating and maintaining a stable writing career (if that's your goal) isn't easy or quick for most authors. These days hiding comfortably in your book-lined study, producing a book a year and only coming out to talk to your agent, or autograph books at launches is a thing of the past. You have to be visible to readers.

While authors have always participated in building their image and brand, today it's more vital than ever to be strategic. It's not enough to let your agent or publisher deal with all the stuff outside of writing.

Everywhere you look it's all about "brand" and "publishing strategies". Which can be overwhelming; too complex to get your head around. Especially when things change so fast.

Traditionally-published authors need to do a lot of their own marketing, manage their own branding. Some even have to run their own blog tours and pay for flights and launches, or arrange reviews with big-name newspapers.

And don't even get me started on how much an indie (self-published) author has to do.

All of it with an eye toward what the market is looking for. Authors seeking a career (read "paid decent money") can start off in one genre and end up in a career back-alley. But they might find a different niche, rebrand themselves and get paid big dollars.

Indie authors have an advantage in that they can move fast, catch the latest trends and ride them, keep up with the latest software and platforms.

Whatever type of writing career you decide on, prepare to change. The readers, the platforms, the markets—they all move on and you need to move as well.

But start with knowing what you truly want out of your writing. Then make the choices that will get you to that goal.

Business of Writing Suggestions:

The industry is changing too quickly to pin down any specific long-lasting strategy. The first sections of this book are just to point you in the right direction and give you a push.

Here are a few thoughts to get you started…

- Attend writers' conferences in genres you like (you'll make great friends). Network with people and authors you admire. Offer to buy them a drink (most authors are happy to sit and chat if someone hands them a whiskey or gin and tonic). Ask (politely) what they did to get where they are today.

- Join some of the social media forums and groups dedicated to author craft and support topics. Lurk and learn what they do—how many hours a day they work, how much marketing they do, whether they are indie or traditionally published and why they chose that option. How many books they write per year. Whether they write to market for income, or for fun, and how they feel about that. Ask questions.

- Once you've filtered their answers, then start deciding where you sit and how that affects what you want to write.

Part 2—Finding Your Style.

Something to Ponder: What genre do you feel most comfortable reading? Is it the same as the one you write?

And so we proceed apace with my verbiage on the parallels between martial arts and writing (or, indeed, any creative industry). As you can see by that opening sentence, I've been watching a lot of Shakespeare recently. Which may seem unconnected to this topic, but actually is related.

Normally I write sci-fantasy, urban fantasy, sci-fi stories. But I gave a *"Fight Like a Girl—Writing Fight Scenes for Female Characters"* workshop at the Romance Writers of Australia conference and it reminded me how much I used to love reading romances. I even wrote a bunch when I was younger. Most were terrible.

I moved on to Speculative fiction writing, because that was where I felt most comfortable. But I still read widely in other genres and enjoy mashing genres up in unexpected ways. It helps to keep my writing fresh and unique. Helps to keep me interested and not jaded.

Martial Arts:

When people first go to a dojo, they often know little about martial arts in general, and less about the differences between various types. Sometimes they join one dojo, hate the style, tar all martial arts with the same brush, and quit.

The more open-minded might hunt around until they find a dojo or sensei or style that suits them, then stick with it. Master it. Become terrifyingly-skilled and powerful in that one style.

Some get to a reasonable level in one art, see the gaps in its curriculum and move on to another art to round out their skillset. Often they end up with a hybrid martial art that's unique to them and fantastically-effective.

It all comes down to knowing yourself and what you want from your art. If you want a martial art that's brutal and immediately practical, then do Jujitsu or Krav Maga. If you want one that's meditative, spiritual, soft, and flowing, then try Tai Chi or Aikikai.

Find what works for you. Find what will work against your anticipated opponent. Master the subtleties of it. Blend it with another art if you like. The important thing is to find a style that suits you and what you want to achieve.

Writing:

In writing (as in all creative arts) it's hard to solidify your "style" or "voice" when you start out. You often begin by mimicking your favourite stories. A lot of great writers started out in fanfic. A lot still write fanfic which is awesome and adored by many thousands of readers across the world.

You might try crime, then decide thriller is more what you love. Or you might be deliberate and find a niche market that's booming in a genre you like. Or you might work in the genre you devoured as a teen and never change because it's fulfilling to write the stories you couldn't find.

The point is, any of those options is fine. Gone are the days when you had to stick to one genre for the rest of your life. You're most welcome to, but if you read widely there's nothing stopping you from writing widely, too. Some readers will follow you, some won't. If you're worried, use different pen names. If you don't care so much, then don't.

(NOTE: I wouldn't recommend writing erotica, horror, and children's books all under the same name.)

Study the genre you love as intensively as a martial artist studies the style they love. Understand its nuances and tropes. Then branch out and master other genres if you want to. Each one will teach you something new.

Thrillers are great for learning pacing and tension. Literary will help with character studies. Romance dives into emotional conflict. Read genres you're unfamiliar with. Use their influence to modify your core love and create something even better.

Something unique.

Something editors haven't seen a thousand times already

Something YOU.

Business of Writing Suggestions:

- Go through your bookshelf, your ebooks, and your library. Pull out the books you loved best and work out what genre they belong to. Are they crime, science-fiction, romance, pure literature, the classics? Are they a mash-up of a couple of genres?

- Research who your target audience is going to be—you'll need to write differently for different ages and genres.

- Now decide if you also want to *write* in one (or more) of those genres. Experiment. Find what flows most smoothly and sounds most natural to you. Start with that one. You can change later if you like. It won't kill your career.

Craft of Writing Suggestions:

- Once you know where to start, go do some research into the 'tropes' and the 'cliches' of that genre. Tropes are just the standard events that happen in a certain genre. For example, a crime novel will usually have a dead body, theft, or bomb at the beginning somewhere. In a romance, a couple will often meet and fall out, meet and fall out several times until getting together at the end. Science fiction will always have high-tech futuristic settings, gadgets, and often spaceships.

    Cliches, on the other hand, are over-used phrases, sentences, or even ideas. Things people are sick of seeing in a story.

- When you know your genre's tropes and clichés, it's easier to put in what's important to your reader and leave out what will annoy your editor.

- Then you can go a step further and learn how to subvert or overturn those tropes to surprise your reader and delight your editor. Because remember, editors and publishers read many thousands of stories every year. You need to find a unique voice AND a unique plot/setting/character to make your story stand out.

Part 3—Co-operation/Collaboration

Something to ponder: Where do you start learning and who do you learn from?

After publishing my 80AD series and having it go a bit viral, I became worried that I wasn't a good enough writer to repeat that success. I lucked out with that first series. To progress, I needed feedback and help. Up until then, I'd been winging it; writing solo. But I wanted to be *better*—and for that I needed teachers.

Martial Arts:

In most martial arts, a student can do a lot of solo training. Many arts have kata (practice movements) that can be done alone. And they're great for training muscle-memory, which leads to quicker reactions.

But for mastery you need other people. Partners. Teachers. Students.

Aikido literally means "*The Way of Peace and Harmony*". (Which is beautifully ironic when you consider how effective it can be as a martial art). Irony aside, the art is both about avoiding confrontation, and about harmonising with your opponent and using their momentum to augment your power.

To learn those things, you need years of training and co-operative people to train with.

Many people look at aikido and complain that the uke (training partner) is *too* co-operative. That uke runs at the nage (person doing the technique) with a hand conveniently offered and never resists the technique being applied.

So, (the trolls say) the resulting throw or lock looks too effortless and beautiful to be effective and wouldn't work in real life.

And it's true that uke doesn't resist. It's true that they sail through the air and fall gracefully; that they leap up and return for more without damage.

What the observer doesn't see is the countless hours spent by both partners learning in co-operation and collaboration. Learning to finely judge timing and force.

Each partner is different and each training session involves learning to read body language, gauge skill levels—and reacting appropriately to apply the right technique in the right way. At the same time, uke is learning to respond to the technique correctly and not get hurt.

These are the yin and yang of martial arts. Both giving and receiving the technique are important skills to master. Both uke and nage learn from each other, no matter what their belt levels are.

To begin with, you feel awkward and clumsy as either uke or nage. The technique only works because someone is jumping at the right time. You suck and your technique sucks. It feels like you'll never throw or fall with beauty and grace and power.

But, eventually, after years of co-operative help and practice, you get it. The moments where it works effortlessly become more frequent. Throws become more powerful. Falls become less painful. Anticipating the next problem/attack becomes easier.

The subtle nuances of locking a human body into organic origami become easier to see and achieve. Teaching others opens new understanding and you improve again.

It's never perfect, but it's a heck of a lot better than when you started. And you don't have to think about it much.

Writing:

How does this relate to writing? After all, authors are often wont to say writing is a solitary art. And it is, in part. You tend to spend long hours frowning over papers or keyboards, attempting to wrestle recalcitrant characters, swearing at pedestrian plots, and ignoring long-suffering partners/children/pets.

But you shouldn't be solitary. Every creative endeavour is the result of a team. Everyone needs external input; help of some sort at some point in their life. A mature writer's work often reads more fluidly and beautifully than a beginning writer's because they've spent years collaborating, co-operating, and learning.

As an adult writer, you first put pen to paper by drawing on the practiced knowledge drilled into us by patient schoolteachers and parents. Then, when you become aware of the gaps in your skill levels, you reach out to mentors, other writers, friends, and ask for feedback, instruction, critiquing.

And *man* does that hurt to start with. Every sentence turns out to be clumsy and ugly. Plot holes abound and you wonder how you could have possibly missed them. You feel like you'll never be a decent writer. There are often tears and swearing.

But slowly, if you don't resist, you learn to incorporate the feedback into new stories from scratch. And the editing/critiquing becomes more about subtleties and nuance than big, clumsy mistakes. Reading and critiquing others' work helps develop your eye for flaws in your own. And a good mentor, who's not arrogant, will learn from you as well.

You're not in this writing gig alone. Be open to learning and let others' experience help you find the best sources of vital skills and craft knowledge.

With the give-and-take of working with others, you approach mastery.

Craft of Writing Suggestions:

- Random internet searches seeking "how to write a novel" can lead you down dark, expensive, and misleading alleys. Instead, find your nearest reputable writers centre. They often have free online resources, good quality workshops, competitions you can enter, links to writers conferences you can attend.

- Seek out other writers. Find your local writers group—or even better, a critique group so you get more than just chats and coffee and friends. Being critiqued by more-skilled writers is the fastest way to learn to create graceful, powerful writing and stories that work in harmony with the reader's imagination.

Don't shy away from good feedback and don't take without giving. Be glad that someone is willing to help you and help them right back.

- If your budget allows, find an award-winning author who writes in your genre and sidelines in mentoring or teaching story development concepts and giving feedback.

- Find a good quality editor asap. When you find one you work well with, hang onto them for dear life. And pay them what they are worth.

  Even if you're considering self-publishing (in fact, *especially*), you'll need an editor. (They can usually be tamed with incentives in the form of chocolate or wine.)

Part 4—Warrior spirit

Something to Ponder: How well can you take rejection/handle pain?

So continues my blathering about the transfer of skills and attitude from one part of my life to another. Whether it resonates with anyone else out there is questionable. Hopefully, yes. Otherwise, well, I'm just enjoying putting my thoughts into order, so bear with me.

Martial Arts:

One of the big things you learn by sticking with martial arts is how to take a few knocks. During my year of intensive training for my first blackbelt, my arms were so covered in bruises that I drew sidelong looks from people in shopping centres. But, to me, they were badges of honour. They hurt, but I'd earned every damned one.

In many ways, physical pain is easier to bear than emotional pain. Might seem obvious, but bruising heals. However, there are few things as painful in life as rejection of one sort or another. Emotional pain often leaves lifelong scars that stop you from progressing—due to fear of being hurt again.

But the act of being knocked down—either physically or emotionally—is one we all go through. Some more than others. And the resilience to get back up, again and again and again, is a learned skill. It does come more easily to some bloody-minded souls than others. But it can be learned by anyone.

(Bearing in mind there are some circumstances where it's physically safer to stay down. That's up to you to judge, not me.)

Martial arts is good at showing you what you can handle. That you can absorb more blows than you thought. That you can learn to be better—as long as you don't give up when you aren't perfect the first time. Or the second.

Once or twice a year we do a hajime class in aikido. Hajime just means 'begin', which is horribly misleading. In fact, the class is two to three hours of unrelenting action, yelling, bruising, throwing, falling, getting up, falling, hurting, getting up. Every technique done a dozen times as fast as you can and at full strength.

Part of the agony is not knowing how long the class will go on for. It's up to sensei to decide when it's over.

I've seen people faint, wake and get back up; or stagger off, vomit, and come back onto the mat, crying but determined to finish. There are also some who leave the mat and don't come back.

Your job is to access that warrior spirit. To dig deep inside and find the reserves and sheer determination to keep getting up even when your legs are jelly, each breath is painful, and your head is spinning.

It's astonishing how far you can push yourself, if you just decide you WILL NOT fucking give up.

Writing:

We are, in our Western-world lives, far too easy on ourselves. Too often we choose the simplest path in an attempt to avoid pain or struggle. And we complain when reaching our goal is difficult. We rail and rant when our crappy first book isn't snapped up in a bidding war between the best publishers. We give up without trying any other path.

This belief—that ideal results should be easy to achieve—is why only 1 in 100 people who start a martial art (or writing a book) continue past the first month. Why only 1 in 1000 who continue past a month make it though to one blackbelt (or one novel).

How did we get to this point? Why do we think achieving our goals should be easy?

It's to do with our mindset. What my sensei calls "spirit".

In an effort to raise our children's self-esteem and confidence, we praise them for simply existing, for being genetically gifted in some way—beauty, speed, intelligence.

In doing so, we do our children a vast disservice. We should praise their tenacity, their determination to learn a new skill, their persistence in gaining each step towards understanding.

Not how easily it came to them or the fact that they even participated.

How impressive their ability to keep getting back up is.

Not how easily they did it the first time.

We need to praise their resilience and warrior spirit.

Not their existence.

Doing so grows adults who can weather hard times. Who can take a publisher's rejection without bitching that the story is "misunderstood". Who can logically weigh up a good editor's suggestions for improvement, instead of taking them as a disparagement of a genetically-gifted talent for writing. Who can keep submitting, even after dozens of rejections.

Who will focus on the process, not the outcomes.

Who will keep working to improve their craft until the acceptances outweigh the rejections.

Find your determination. Find your warrior spirit. Keep getting up, even after your heart is bruised and your ego is mashed.

Instead of seeking recognition for perfection, seek the will of the warrior-scholar.

Seek to learn and grow. Doing so is a reward in itself, but will also help you along the path to your end-goal, whatever that is.

Business of Writing Suggestions:

- Research the major (5 or so) publishing houses. Read their websites. See what they like to publish and what they refuse/will reject. Look at who their big-star writers are and decide if you like what they publish or if it doesn't fit your tastes.

- Also study expected novel word lengths. For example, if you want to traditionally publish, most publishers won't take a 300 000 word fantasy novel from a new author. 120 000 words is about the maximum.

- Research the major e-magazines that publish short stories in your genre. If you want to get a traditional novel publishing contract, you'll find it easier to get a foot in the door if you have a proven track record of high quality short stories.

  Writing short stories is also a great path to learning the craft techniques.

- Study the guidelines for both novel and short story submissions. Most publishers and e-mags will list what they want their manuscripts to look like (eg: what fonts to use, spacing, how to indicate scene changes etc).

  If you breach those guidelines, your story won't be read at all. You may as well get a headstart by formatting your manuscript correctly.

- Just be prepared for LOT of rejections to start with. Don't panic. You're not the only one. Every author gets rejections—even the most rich and famous.

  Often it's just because your story doesn't suit the theme of the anthology or magazine, or is too similar to one they've already accepted.

Get up from the mat, dust yourself off. Write more, send more out, and the rejections will hurt less because you'll be less emotionally-attached to the stories.

Part 5—Adaptability

Something to Ponder: How defensive are you about your writing? How open to change are you? How hard are you trying to live up to perceived expectations?

I've been exhausted this week and when I'm tired, I'm likely to bull straight through a task without considering other ways of doing it. I just want things to work the first time without me having to think.

I also tend to get angry with myself and defensive of work I've done; less likely to listen to good advice, or change what's written because I'm too tired to put in the effort required.

Not great when you're a writer and your job is to be original and interesting.

Martial Arts:

The martial art of Aikido has often been likened to water. Not only because the movements are fluid (which they are), but because water doesn't resist—it wraps around, turns aside, redirects. Adapts. Aikido is never about resisting because that's about strength.

There's always someone stronger. That's one of the things I love about the art. It's actually an advantage to be small, because the *only* way to make a technique work on someone bigger and stronger is to do it correctly. Force is useless.

One of my senseis literally felt like a jellyfish when you grabbed his arm. The harder you grabbed, the harder you punched, the more relaxed he became. The more he adapted to your grip.

Then suddenly you'd be on your back seeing stars, with no idea how you got there, and wondering how soon it would be before you could breathe again.

Once I learned the concept—being tense resulted in worse technique, but relaxed resulted in better technique—it became fun to try it out on the bigger, stronger (less-openminded) whitebelt guys in our dojo.

The tighter they grabbed, the more I relaxed. Then…wham, they were on the floor blinking up in astonishment. Funny how much more willing to learn from a small female they often were after that.

Being rigid and resisting adaption, using anger or brute-forcing something, insisting that your way is the only and best way…those are a fool's game.

It always ends badly, for someone.

Writing:

Writing is also about being adaptable. Not only being prepared to grow and learn new skills—as mentioned earlier—but also in what kind of writer you are.

You may have heard that, when it comes to writing a book, there are "pantsers" and "planners". The meanings are reasonably self-evident.

Pantsers "fly by the seat of their pants" and write whatever comes to mind, going with the flow, letting the characters run the story.

Planners plot out scenes and whole novels in advance then write from scene to scene with specific goals in mind.

Of course there are degrees of each as well. Some are more hardcore planners than others.

Neither is right or wrong. Both methods are completely fine. Do what feels right to you.

Too often, people try to squeeze pantsers into a plan and force planners to be spontaneous. If someone's insisting you do one or the other, please ignore them.

But both (whether they admit it or not) have to be adaptable. (The planners may have a harder time with this than the pantsers do.)

The real key is to just relax. The more uptight you get, the worse your writing will be. The more you worry about whether you're doing it "right" the more stilted your words will come out. Relax, adapt.

Experiment with a few different ways of doing things.

Change the plot or the character, or the setting, if you need to. Hell, change the whole world. You can do that, you know.

Don't force a plot or character into a set mould just because that's the way you planned it. Allow things to change if they serve the story's interest best. And don't force yourself to plan a story if doing so kills the joy for you.

But, if you're a planner to the core, don't sit there and try to force spontaneity. That's an oxymoron.

You might even find you fall somewhere in the middle—a bit of pantsing, a bit of planning.

There is no "right" way to write. All the rules you've read are just guidelines to point you in the right direction—the end of your novel or story. But you can take your own path. Flow with your own creativity. Adapt to suit yourself and your readers. Imagine your ideal reader and write for yourself and for them.

The most important thing is: RELAX and stop trying to cram yourself into some mental image of the "ideal" writer.

Craft of Writing Suggestions:

- Research different types of novel/story structures. A novel's structure is really just the path followed by the plot (also known as the narrative conflict or external conflict). The action that happens to the protagonist/s. There are several forms. Read and compare. See if any of them fit the type of story you like to write.

  If you're a pantser, that might help you spot plot holes. If you're a planner it might help you feel comfortable that the plan for your novel is hitting the right sweet spots. Or show you why you've got a saggy middle.

- Research Archetypal Characters and decide whether you have them in your story, or whether you're happy to leave them out altogether. Do they fit your genre? Will your readers be bothered if they are missing? Will you be bothered?

Part 6—Big things and Small

Something to Ponder: Are you seeing the big picture or are you focussed on the minutiae? As a writer you need to understand both.

I've been trying to catch up on the myriad of small, important things that have to happen in life. The "Important but Not Urgent" stuff (to quote *7 Habits of Highly Effective People*). Which led me to remember the scale from Big to Small that happens when you're learning new skills.

Martial Arts

In martial arts, you start off with gross movements: this foot goes here, this hand goes here, now move this way. No, not that way, *this* way.

It's like learning to walk all over again—complete with falling down. A lot.

The point is, you start with the big motor control movements. You feel like an elephant. No, more like a completely uncoordinated sloth. Then, as you progress and you get those first motions imprinted into muscle-memory, you stop having to think about them.

They just happen. Sometimes when you don't mean for them to happen. (Note to self: don't elbow well-meaning friends who try to get your attention by grabbing you from behind.)

Then your sensei or senior training partner starts adjusting middle-sized things—the angle of your arm, the depth of your stance, where your energy is focussed, the alignment of your hips.

And you get better at those until you don't have to think about them, either.

Then your instructors start in on the little things—the angle of your wrist and fingers, the exact timing of when to grab an arm and turn; the awareness of where your partner's foot is when you throw; recognising the feeling of when a throw or lock is perfect.

The subtle things that cement power and fluidity into your technique.

The things that make it look effortless to the outsider while your uke (partner) feels like they've been hit by a truck. It takes years and the learning never, actually ends. You can always improve.

But... the crucial thing is that you *must* start by mastering the Big things before the medium and small. The latter won't work if the former are all out of whack.

Writing:

Writing is similar, but most of us start by just...writing. We often have no mentor, so we just launch straight into a novel or short story.

If we're determined and resilient, when the stories aren't accepted we look for why we got knocked back. Why did the 300 000 word fantasy novel get rejected by the major publishers? Why did the 90 000 word romance with eight POV characters and twelve unresolved subplots get declined?

In doing so, we discover what's considered an acceptable story/novel length by publishing companies. Or how to properly format a short story.

Or we learn the big issues that make a novel feel "right" to a reader or editor—story structure for Western culture novels (yes, Western society novels are structured differently than those from other cultures). How short stories work. Character arcs. Thematic ideas.

It's overwhelming to start with. There are so many new concepts. But you get it eventually and your stories slide into correct structure (mostly) without effort.

You then learn the middle sized things—scene structure, pacing, character voices, wrangling subplots.

Finally you tackle the details—the use of language to manipulate emotion, the structure of sentences, metaphors, poetic devices, purposeful word choices.

All of these things, (with more, obviously) are what make your finished product appear fluid and powerful; effortlessly beautiful.

It can take years and the learning never ends. Or it shouldn't. You can always find ways to improve.

But... the crucial thing is that you *must* start by mastering the big things before the medium and small. The latter won't work if the former are out of whack.

Craft of Writing Suggestions:

- Following on from the previous module's suggestion...If you're writing genre fiction, you'll probably find most novels fit the Three Act Play structure. If you're comfortable using that format, dive more deeply into understanding it.

- To start, learn where the key Turning Points for the major plot/external conflict should appear in a novel. Learn the words for each point eg: Establishing Normal, Inciting Incident, Point of No Return, Mid-point Reversal/Mirror moment, Darkest Hour, Climax, Denouement.

- Now work out what you're trying to achieve with each of those scenes. And how to fill in the bits between them.

- Usually subplots help to keep things ticking along in between the major turning points. Subplots have their own matching structure and similar plot points. They just pop up in between the major plot points to keep things racing along and avoid mid-story sag.

- Research Story Beats (which may or may not be the same as a Turning Point, depending on your genre)

- Watch a few movies and critique their structure to see what makes them work or fail. Big Hollywood movies are useful because their turning point locations in the film can been timed to the minute.

   Do the same with a few books. See if they hit the major turning points in the right places. Or are there sections that feel rushed or slow because the book/movie inserted or left out scenes?

- Then research Short Story structure because that's a whole different ballgame. But short stories are a great place to practice your craft. You can also send them off to anthologies and e-magazines. You'll get rejections but some sites will also give you little snippets of feedback.

Part 7—Self-Discipline

Something to Ponder: Are you prepared to do what's right over what's easy? Do you have the ability to start things you're afraid of and finish things that seem impossible?

Sometimes you have those weeks where you look at the pile of tasks and go "stuff it, I'm going to watch a movie." And sometimes that's fine. We all need a break. You can't push yourself constantly.

But keep in mind whether you're doing it out of reluctance to try and fail rather than true tiredness.

Martial Arts.

Aikido is derived from samurai arts, and maintains many of the traditions of strict dojo etiquette. There is a lot of kneeling in seiza, bowing, shutting up, showing you've understood by saying "osu".

People who lack focus and discipline, who lack warrior spirit in gradings (ie: do a grading halfheartedly), who are disrespectful to Sensei, to other students, or the dojo… they generally don't last long.

Because all of those require a measure of self-discipline to learn and stick with—especially the shutting up.

Then there's the daily self-discipline. In aikido, it takes an average of 3 years to get to the first black belt. And it's not three years of one class per week.

To get from brown to my first black, I trained around 19x1hour classes each week, for a year. My arms, legs and often ribs were purple and black. My ankles and wrists were often twisted and swollen. I went to sleep picturing techniques and practiced movements at work and at home.

Believe me, though, many days were a huge test of willpower just to get in the car and leave my driveway. Especially in winter when it was dark and cold and staying home was *so* much easier and warmer.

But I wanted the knowledge, skill, and self-respect more than I wanted to watch TV.

That's what the first blackbelt really indicates: you've shown you're disciplined enough to suck up your ego, to overcome your urge to do the easy thing, and to finish what you started.

Writing:

Writing is not dissimilar for the dedicated author. There are traditions to know, novels and stories to be completed, behaviours to avoid, shutting up to do, respect to show.

All of those take self-discipline. As does the effort needed to learn the craft skills. And the restraint needed not to rant at another author, or a reader who's left you a bad review. So, too, the awareness required to know when you should listen to what more experienced industry professionals have to say.

Seeking validation by talking too much about what you know is easy. Shutting up is not.

(By the way, I'm not saying I'm perfect at it. We're all guilty of wanting validation, and of sounding like know-it-alls or idiots sometimes.)

In addition, there's the everyday self-discipline. To complete a novel takes work. Every day, if possible. It takes discipline to write when you don't feel like it. To write when it's not working. To write when people are telling you to go do something that sounds way more fun in the short term.

And, when the novel is done, you must put aside ego and send it off to experienced beta readers (not just your dad or mum). And, later, to an editor. Once you've shelved your resentment at their advice, that's when you start learning how to refine your technique as a writer.

Completing your first novel (including editing and beta readers etc) is roughly the equivalent to a first brown belt. It will take self-discipline to come back to the keyboard, learn more, and create the next masterpiece.

But if you want the knowledge, skill, and self-respect that comes from finishing something difficult, then it's worth the effort and the discipline.

Now go put fingers to keyboard and take the next steps towards your writing blackbelt.

Craft of Writing Suggestions:

- Now that you've done some research into story structure, discipline yourself to sit down and make your novel the best it can be.

- The first suggestion is (if you haven't done this already): FINISH THE BOOK. You can't fix or edit an unfinished novel. Most people who start a novel don't finish.

Even if the book never gets published, just finishing it will give you an endorphin rush and do wonders for your self-confidence. You'll also learn a lot.

- If you're not sure how to finish it, or just plain have writers block, call in reinforcements. Go to a workshop. Brainstorm with your writers group buddies.

Brainstorming is a lot of fun. You'll either get fantastic new ideas for your novel, or new ideas you can set aside to use in some other novel. Or you'll get clearer insight into what is truly important for you to say in this novel and that will help you push past the block.

- If you're writing a book requiring intensive worldbuilding, start thinking now about the GRAPES of the world (Geography, Religion, Achievements, Politics, Economy, Social Structure). NOTE: I'd add 'Infrastructure' as well.

These things *should* have effects on your plot and characters. And getting the world's culture and infrastructure worked out will give you new plot ideas to help finish the story.

- Also consider drawing a rough map. It will help with continuity—eg: how many days it takes characters to travel from town A to town B. If you're writing fantasy, you may want to hire a cartographer as well and get them to draw you a really pretty map to go in the book when it's done. Publishing companies don't do that for you.

- Please, please, please do your research as well. It's incredibly frustrating for a reader if a book contains basic errors of geography, history, occupational information etc. The more thorough your research is, the less likely your reader is to throw the book across the room in irritation.

Part 8—Proving Yourself

Something to Ponder: How much external validation do you need?

Most people need validation from others to some degree or another. It's part of being a tribal animal. But it's also potentially damaging.

Martial Arts:

One of the things I love about Yoshinkan Aikido is the lack of competitions. No trophies, no 'best of'. Just a focus on improving your own skill—nothing on proving yourself better than anyone else.

Even the belt system reflects that. You're a white belt for 7 gradings—right up until you're a brown belt (3 brown levels with no stripes). Then you're black.

Even with that attitude in the art, there's always at least one person with a desperate desire to prove themselves. It's really insecurity, but usually manifests as arrogance, or bullying, or bravado.

White and brown belts, generally don't yet have the finesse to make a technique work without using brute strength. So that's what the insecure student will resort to in an attempt to prove they can *make* it work.

Often that leads to a subtle revenge war between junior training partners. A kind of *"you hurt me so I'll hurt you back to prove I can do it, too"* type of interaction.

Unfortunately, as one of the few female senior blackbelts in my dojo, encountering one of these trainees was often challenging.

Sometimes they were males that resented learning from a woman for whatever reason. Sometimes they just didn't believe I could throw them, and would resist the technique to prove I couldn't.

I could, but it would have involved breaking their arm or dislocating their shoulder.

Luckily, my ego's never been so fragile that I had to hurt someone to prove I was better. And one of Aikido's central tenets is *Avoid the Falling Rock,* ie: avoid danger and conflict where possible.

So, I would simply swap training partners. Let them think what they like. I didn't need to prove my worth or capability.

Belittling someone and being competitive to make yourself look better is a pointless tribal dominance game that results in nothing but pain, resentment, and anger.

Many people are caught up in that cycle, though, so it's good to be aware it exists. And to be aware of how you handle it as a martial artist, as a writer, and as a person.

Writing:

Those same dominance/proving yourself games exist in the writing world as well. One trap we all fall into is the comparison spiral. It begins when you start comparing your writing, your book sales, your book cover, your number "likes" on social media, etc etc, to those of another writer.

By all means, study what they do and learn from them. But don't compare and get upset based on how you both write, what you both write, or how successful you both are.

Believe me, every writer is hiding their own insecurities behind shiny, colourful masks of success and popularity.

Everyone knows something that you don't. Find out their story, their skill, what makes them unique and special. Be happy for them. Encourage and praise them. Learn from them. They're not your competitor.

You don't have to prove you're better. Lift them up, don't tear them down.

Craft of Writing Suggestions:

- Find a novel or story by your favourite love-to-hate successful author. Put aside your bruised ego and study the novel closely. See if you can learn what they do and how they do it.

- The next step to this process is to go through and look for a few things.
    - Have you started your story in the right place (ie: close to the exciting bit where things begin to happen) Work out the best scene that's close to the action but still gives the reader a chance to fall into your world smoothly without feeling overwhelmed. No point in writing 30 000 words only to find later you started the whole story too far from where it really gets interesting.

    - Do all your characters have a Growth Arc (either positive or negative or flat)? If you're not sure what a growth arc is, now's a great time to go research it and make sure every key character has one. It's sometimes also called the Internal Conflict.

There's a lot more, but we'll do those in the upcoming modules.

Part 9—Fear & self doubt

Something to Ponder: Are you letting fear hold you back?

This week I've been suffering—as many of us do—with self-doubt. Is my writing good enough? Why isn't this easier? Maybe my stories aren't being read by enough people because my writing really is terrible.

Our brains are horrible to us.

Many of us are afraid. Afraid to hurt other people. Afraid of being hurt. Afraid to try in case we fail. Afraid to throw ourselves into things in case it proves we'll never be good enough.

Martial Arts:

This fear is especially obvious when you get women on the dojo mat. It becomes painfully clear how socialised they are not to hurt people; not to be physically resilient; not to believe they are capable of mastering something as potentially lethal as a martial art. Of course, many men suffer from similar doubts and fears.

Women hit you, then either giggle nervously, or apologise and look horrified—or both. It takes ages to stop that habit.

They'll rarely throw a full-strength punch. They normally have to be taught how to punch correctly, whereas men require less encouragement and less training in that area.

When women take the first few hits, they'll usually gasp and retreat, wide-eyed. For many it's the first time they've ever been struck and they don't know how to react. Sadly, for others it's not and they shrink back in fear.

The women who stick with the training often end up better than men because they can't use strength to make techniques work. They have to do it right, with power instead of brute force. And that, in turn, gives them a sliver of extra confidence.

Eventually, both men and women overcome many of the fears and self-doubts they carried when they first stepped on the mat. A grading system offers a clear path toward their end goal.

Mastering a martial art can do that—give people a basic self-belief that can be critical in times of stress and fear. A firm grounding to stand on.

In a true fight, self-doubt and fear will cause you to hesitate and you will lose the fight before you even start.

And only training, learning, encouragement, and repeated experience in overcoming obstacles embeds the confidence people need, to believe they are capable of more than they thought.

Writing:

In writing it's not always so clear when you're improving and succeeding. There are no coloured belts to achieve. It takes every writer time and practice, and repeated experience overcoming obstacles to conquer their instinctive fear of not being good enough—of being judged unworthy.

Even the best writers admit they, too, experience bouts of self-doubt. It's normal, but they don't let it cripple them or stop them writing.

We are a tribal animal. We rely on feedback to know our place in the tribe and to survive as a group. Self-doubt is hardwired into our brains as part of our need to fit in and survive.

Accept that you'll never completely overcome it. Understand why it's there. Let it go as a pointless waste of time.

You'll never be perfect. Accept that.

Instead of wallowing in your doubts, use them as a springboard to improve your skills. Learn from your doubts, but don't let them stop you from writing.

Every new skill you learn *is* improving your writing, even if you can't see it and don't get a grading certificate.

Writer's Life Suggestions:

- Make a list of all the things you believe about yourself or your writing and examine the truth of them with a bit more emotional distance. Think about the things you habitually tell yourself eg: 'I'll never get a publisher.' Or 'My stories just aren't as good as hers.'

    Are your beliefs about yourself real? Most of the time they aren't. They're the result of parental or societal conditioning. They're also often common misbeliefs that many people hold. They can be overcome.

- Take that list and decide which of the beliefs you want to work on. Think you're no good at dialogue or characterisation? Find writing classes to take on those topics. Feel like your writing is amateurish?

Look back at your older stories to see how far you've come.

- Not sure you are affecting your readers in a meaningful way? Don't be afraid to write deep, complex themes into every type of story and novel. Authors are often afraid of being labelled as 'preachy' so they leave out or misuse the concept of "Theme".

  But the most satisfying stories are ones that bind together the Plot (external conflict) with the Character Arc (internal conflict) AND the Theme. Ideally, all three should be connected and affect each other. The theme should underlie each scene, each subplot, and each decision the character makes. Not in a preachy way, just subtly.

  Track down some information about the interconnection between Plot, Character Arcs, and Theme.

- Work out what themes are 'universal' and will appeal to all your readers. Things like fear, self-doubt, anxiety, desire for approval, need for control, desire for admiration/respect etc. Those are the ones that will give the most satisfying 'feel' to your story.

And, as you're learning about those themes, you may find exploring them through your characters helps you overcome some of your own misbeliefs about yourself as a writer.

Part 10—Commitment.

Something to Ponder: How serious are you; how committed to writing good stories?

This has been one of those 'why the heck am I doing this weeks'. You know what I mean. When you doubt you can write, you doubt anyone gives a crap about what you write, you doubt whether it's all 'worth it', you wonder if you'll ever feel like a successful author.

I had to remind myself that all authors have days like that. Sometimes weeks, or months.

Then I had to remind myself: those moments are really about commitment. How committed are you, really, to achieving whatever goal you set yourself?

Martial Arts:

In martial arts training, a lack of commitment by the uke (partner/attacker) causes problems for the nage (defender/person performing the technique). And visa versa. Most injuries happen when uke doesn't attack hard, or because nage doesn't throw with full intent.

Sometimes nage panics and lets go too early in the throw, preventing uke from learning to fall correctly. Or uke lets go (or doesn't jump properly) out of fear of being injured, preventing nage from learning how to do the technique.

In training, both partners have to commit to the technique or risk failure or injury.

And, in an actual attack, if the victim doesn't commit fully to fighting back—with the awareness they will have to both take and give damage—he/she will most certainly lose.

Commitment to training, to the technique, or to do damage for survival is a mindset. One that has to be learned by most people. After all, it's far easier to walk away from difficult circumstances than it is to master the techniques that will resolve the situation. And yes, sometimes walking away is the right thing to do.

But sometimes committing wholeheartedly to making something work (a relationship, a career, a martial arts technique) is better.

Harder, but better.

Writing:

Once you've decided you want to write that novel / get that publishing deal / get short stories into professionally paid magazines / etc, then it will take commitment to achieve that goal. You can't half-arse it and expect to reach your target.

You need to be committed to growing as a person and learning as an artist. That will help you write better, understand other people better, and create richer, deeper characters. But, most of all, you must commit to doing the work. To not walking away with it incomplete.

You have to start the novel *and* finish it. Then get feedback *and* apply it. Then ruthlessly self-edit again and 'kill your darlings', often removing your favourite scenes, dialogue, or even characters.

Then get editors, develop a thick skin and accept your writing isn't perfect (taking damage to your ego, possibly). Then spend the time finding agents or publishers or learning how to self-publish *and* handle rejections and bad reviews you might get.

At any step, you can quit, of course. Walk away. Say it's all too hard and not worth the effort.

But if you really want to achieve your writing goals, you have to accept that you will take a certain amount of mental and emotional damage along the way. And you have to commit to the process of getting better at everything, following all the steps, and hanging on for dear life until you reach your goal.

If you're going to jump into this hobby/career, then jump wholeheartedly, with full commitment to being the best you can in order to achieve whatever goal you've set yourself.

Which is easier said than done, I know. Often the goal can seem unattainable. Especially when you can't see the path to get there. The easiest method is to take your eyes *off* the huge final goal.

It's too distant.

Try focussing, instead, on the first step you need to take.

Want to have a published novel? Step 1: Commit to sitting down every day and writing—even if it's just a few words. Whatever you can manage. Try keeping a journal to stay accountable. Ask a writing buddy to help you.

Much like your characters in your book, the path to attaining your end can be fraught with obstacles, disappointments, people trying to discourage or stop you, side paths that distract you.

It's vital to keep an eye on your level of commitment to your craft and your goal.

Just like it's vital for your characters to keep an eye on their goal and commit to achieving it. The world won't save itself; the hero won't fall in love with the heroine if she quits and runs away from the relationship; the murder won't get solved if the detective gives up.

Craft of Writing Suggestions:

- Consider your character's inner growth arc/internal conflict vs the external conflict. How committed are the characters to achieving their goal? Have you made things hard enough for them, or chickened out because you like the character and can't stand to hurt them? Let them take damage. Let them learn and grow. Make life tough for them so the reward at the end of the story is a bigger payoff.

- Characters who are committed to their goals experience new things, push through hardship, and grow as a result. Their growth makes reading a story enjoyable and interesting. Character stagnation is usually tedious, angst-ridden and often depressing.

- Go back through the story and see if you can strengthen each scene by making the character's decisions reflect their inner conflict and influence their outer conflict. Shake their commitment then renew it, over and over.

- If you're not sure how to do that, take a break and go research how to write a strong inner conflict (character arc) / outer conflict (Plot) connection so the two are tightly bound to each other.

Part 11—Body Awareness.

Something to Ponder: Are you aware of the modern writing "rules" for genre fiction? Or how the modern "rules" differ from older ones?

The last week or so has been tiring—especially for an introvert. A people-y writers conference (great, but tiring), Christmas parties etc. Eventually, I had to just stop, listen to my body, and say 'Nope, staying home today.'

Martial Arts:

In martial arts, learning to control and listen to your body, then adapt your skills to suit is crucial. A dojo might teach a technique the same way to everyone, but that doesn't mean it will work for you the way it works for the guy next to you.

Trying to do it exactly the same will, in fact, lead to frustration and poor skills.

Every person is unique in how they move, how their body works (or doesn't), their speed, muscularity, flexibility etc.

My husband has extremely inflexible joints but mine are hyper-flexible. Our actions to perform techniques are different to compensate. Things that work easily on him have no effect on me, and visa versa.

You may have physical limitations that mean the technique needs to be modified to suit your body. Perhaps your knees are dodgy, or you have shoulder injuries. If doing a technique physically hurts (beyond just a twinge), then stop and find a new way to achieve the result you want without damaging your body.

Ignoring a small amount of pain is good as it teaches you to push through inconvenience to achieve your goal. Ignoring extreme pain is stupid and will result in permanent damage.

Don't let pain and discomfort or limitations hold you back. Just learn to listen to your body and adapt. One of the best martial artists in my dojo had only one arm.

Writing:

You'll get handed a lot of "rules". Many of those are helpful and will improve your writing if you're an emerging author—even if having them pointed out as missing in your manuscript is distressing. Ignore that pain. It's minor and important to push through.

Definitely don't write off your editor and arrogantly dismiss their suggestions for improvement. That would be like ignoring your multi-blackbelt sensei.

BUT...

Think of the "rules" as the martial arts techniques. Once you understand and can apply them properly, *then* listen to your gut and do what serves your story best.

Sometimes "telling" is the best way to get from one scene to the next without tediously "showing" a long trip across boring deserts.

Sometimes a passively written sentence will get across an idea better than an actively written one.

But you can't break the "rules" until you know how to write them properly in the first place.

Use a "wrong" way *if* it's vital to the story. And with the awareness that it might not work; that you might have to experiment with something else.

Even more importantly, be aware of your body's reactions when you're *reading.* If you want to learn how to build tension in a story, read a thriller and take note of when you feel the twist in your stomach. Then stop and re-read the passage to see how the writer did that. If you're reading a drama and find yourself crying, stop and re-read to see why you got so emotional.

Paying attention to your body's reactions when you read will help you become a better writer. And once you understand the "rules" you'll be able to modify the techniques to suit your story and be deliberate about how you guide your readers' emotions.

Craft of Writing Suggestions:

- Start a list of modern genre-writing "rules" or standards. Basically a list of what modern readers are likely to find comfortable to read, as opposed to how the classics and older stories were written.

- Learning these "rules" and applying them (along with basic grammar rules) will help you produce the *best possible* manuscript before you send it to any publishers or editors. That's one of the big keys to acceptance by a publisher, or to successful self-publishing—creating the best possible manuscript.

- Here's a couple of core writing concepts to get you started. Research these and see what you come up with.

- POV (Point of View)—find out the difference between Omniscient Narrator, 3rd Person POV, 3rd person Close POV, 1st Person POV, 1st Person Close POV. Each one will generate a different feeling in the reader. Understanding them will help you decide which to choose for your novel/story.
- Research how to write an Unreliable Narrator and how that would affect which POV you choose
- Understand the "Free Direct Style" of writing a character's internal monologue/thinking as it creates a more immersive experience for the reader—especially the reader of Close 1st person stories.
- Understand 'headhopping' and which POV uses it best.
- Then read a few of the older stories from the early 20th C and back into the classics. See how their use of POV differs to modern stories in the same genre.

Part 12—Old Techniques and New; Good and Bad

Something to Ponder: What older writing styles and "rules" are you unconsciously employing? Are they the best option for modern readers?

This week I've had some interesting discussions with my sensei from the first dojo I attended. We were chatting about the difference between older and newer styles of martial arts. And about whether older techniques should be modified to suit modern expectations.

Which made me stop and think about older vs newer writing styles—a topic I touched on briefly in the previous module.

Martial arts:

After trying other arts, one of the things that made me stay with Yoshinkan Aikido—and the particular sensei and dojo—was the adherence to the older techniques.

The art itself is based on the old empty-handed samurai unarmed combat moves. They are often brutal and based on survival. Which means they are effective even in modern circumstances. Not perfect—no art is. But they contain enough practicality to be useful, even today.

However they have limitations in the modern world. They are nastier than is usually acceptable. Modern laws frown on snapping people's elbows because they've jostled you in a crowd.

The second dojo I attended (after I moved to a different city) retained the older techniques, but also added variations adapting them to modern situations, modern laws, and societal expectations.

It took me a while to adjust, and sometimes I found the newer techniques restrictive because they felt 'soft' and didn't have the same power as the older ones.

But, in truth, that was mostly my perception, rather than reality. Once I let go of that belief, my skills improved to the next level.

Both the older techniques and the modern version had things I could learn. Ways of manipulating my partner's body, or influencing his centre and power, or upsetting his balance. Both had merit. Both were useful.

Some were better than others. But you can learn a lot from unworkable techniques as well.

Learning all of them gave me greater skill and awareness of how to control an attacker; of what would and wouldn't work.

It's worth learning both the older and the newer techniques. Then you can choose which circumstances require which response.

Writing:

When we first write, we often unconsciously include writing styles we grew up reading and loving. But do they suit your modern audience?

Both the older and newer styles of writing have merit. Why do you think people still love Shakespeare and Chaucer, even after 500+ years?

You can learn a lot from reading the classics. The older literature (Jane Austen, Byron, Lovecraft, Poe, Maugham, Alcott, etc) will help you write more lyrically, more emotively, with more complex sentences and beautiful word choices.

Don't be afraid to draw on the older styles if they will suit some aspect of your story. But also be aware of what was bad about them: attitudes of the time that aren't acceptable now; writing styles of the time that would jar on modern readers.

Reading truly terrible books can also help you work out good writing techniques from bad, and teach you how to critically analyse stories.

Once you know what techniques work and why, pick and choose the ones that will suit your story and your readers' ear.

Perhaps you have a semi-immortal character who grew up in the Regency Era. Or are writing historical romance. You can indicate that by choosing dialogue and inner monologue with words and sentence structures suited to the 1830's.

Perhaps you're writing a time-travel scene set 500 years ago. You might need to draw from Shakespeare and adapt your writing to help immerse the reader into that era. Though I wouldn't advise writing full-on faux-Shakespearean. He was, after all, writing plays in iambic pentameter, not real conversations.

The point is to be discerning and selective. Don't throw in only modern techniques because you think they are "rules" of writing. Choose with care and with an eye to how it will influence the story and the reader.

Craft of Writing Suggestions:

- Read a dozen or more classics and older stories across several genres. Take note of sentences that move you, or jar you. Note character dialogue that makes you laugh or cry or feel nothing. Note setting descriptions that create vivid pictures or leave a blank.

Think about why—is it your own prejudices or are the older writing styles just not going to suit your story or your audience? Can you use some of the language to build a unique culture for your novel, or a unique character, or indicate the era and country your story is set in?

- Pick a dozen authors—classics and modern—and write short stories in their voice/style. Don't copy their stories, just their voice/style. It will help you learn how they influence readers, how they use rhythm and word choices, and help you find your own voice.

Love horror? Try writing a story in Lovecraft's voice or Edgar Allan Poe's. Love historical romance? Write like Jane Austen. Love swashbuckling crime? Try Leslie Charteris's *The Saint* series. Love drama, try Ernest Hemingway's *The Old Man and the Sea*. They're all very different voices and you'll learn something useful from each one.

- Pick up some dreadful books (there are a lot out there, many published by big publishing companies). Read them critically, looking for bits that work and bits that don't. Make notes. Discuss with your writers group exactly *why* they don't work. Then don't repeat those mistakes in your own writing.

Part 13—Understanding People

Something to Ponder: Are you able to accept people as they are and see the world from their viewpoint? It's an essential skill for authors.

Let's face it, people are both incomprehensible and fairly predictable. It's a maddening dichotomy that causes much angst. We (unconsciously) expect people to think and behave as we would, then are astonished, blindsided, and often angry when they don't.

One of the most important skills you can have as a martial artist and as a writer is the ability to put yourself into someone else's head. (Not literally—unless, perhaps, you're a horror writer doing hands-on research. Ew!) To understand *why* they choose to think and behave a certain way.

Martial Arts:

As a martial artist, you develop the habit of watching not only your dojo partners, but people around you when you're off the mat and in the "real" world. You scan them up and down and observe how they move, where they move, who they avoid, what they are watching. You analyse their behaviour as individuals and in groups and predict what they might do next.

It's a useful habit even if they aren't a threat. People usually give away their next action in their body language and facial expression.

In fact, it's quite hard *not* to judge and anticipate behaviour based on how people look, speak and act. As a troupe animal, humans rely on reading their companions' moods and reactions in order to adjust their own behaviour to fit in with the troupe (and therefore survive).

A good martial art teaches reading people for a slightly different purpose—to deliberately neutralise or avoid threats before they emerge.

But to do that, you must comprehend and accept how people are likely to act and react in stressful situations.

And that, on its own, is an invaluable skill to master.

Writing:

As a writer, it's vital to dispassionately understand people. Because the more you learn to anticipate how people will behave in any given circumstance, the more you'll be able to write people who aren't YOU onto the page.

If you would never dream of cutting someone off in traffic or working 80 hour weeks—because you're just a super-chill, easy-going person—then you'll have difficulty writing an aggressive workaholic. If you are an anxious introvert who is completely happy never leaving home and never being drawn into any sort of human interaction, then you'll have difficulty writing a fun-loving extroverted party animal who loves being around people 24-7.

You don't have to *be* the characters you write. You just have to deliberately study how other people think and behave. Which results in the ability to write a wider variety of characters that act in ways consistent to their own, unique personalities.

And, as an awesome side-effect, it might even help you be more accepting and tolerant of people you love but perhaps sometimes get on your nerves. Or people you've just never understood before.

Let's face it, any extra tolerance and acceptance is a great thing in today's world.

Our way of thinking and behaving is not the only way. Nor necessarily the right way. Learning how other people think can only be a good thing.

Craft of Writing Suggestions:

- Do some research into creating unique characters—especially into different personality types and their behaviours under stress.

- Order a few books on personality types, on psychology, on human behaviour. Use them to create a varied team of characters that each think differently from you and from your protagonist. Use their differences to generate conflict, humour, and co-operation between the characters.

- Try writing vignettes of each character's life. Just a short scene that shows how they would react under stress, or fear, or joy, or sadness. What key/unique words would they use in dialogue? What physical actions would they perform that reveal how they feel? What body language would show their emotional state?

Part 14—Awareness

Something to Ponder: How much do you (or your characters) see around you and how much do you filter out?

This section follows closely on from the previous one about understanding people—and the one about body awareness—but focuses on world-awareness.

Our brains are actually incapable of keeping everything our eyes see. Instead, we 'filter' the world based on what we're interested in, what we're looking for, what we're afraid of etc.

Martial Arts:

I'm sure many have heard the term *awareness* before. In martial arts, it's about how cognizant you are of yourself, your surroundings, other people, potential dangers etc. Not all arts teach it consciously or deliberately.

But if you're a long-time practitioner, it creeps into your skillset, anyway.

Everyone filters their world based on what they're most interested in and focussed on. If you're training 20 hours a week plus, then your mind becomes focussed on martial arts concepts and that colours your world.

Your balance improves—you stumble and stub your toes less often. Your peripheral vision improves and you often bring up a hand or arm automatically to ward off a motion you hadn't consciously recognised yet.

You learn to act on your 'gut feelings' about people and environments. You note where exits are, where potential problems and weapons are, where blockages and slippages might occur. Even where fire extinguishers or hiding places are.

Many martial artists find their other senses improve as well—they notice unusual smells, or unexpected sounds they previously would have filtered out or ignored.

I was once in a busy shopping centre and my husband (whom I wasn't expecting) snuck up behind me and put a hand on my hip. But I didn't strike with an elbow, (as I normally would) in automatic response. As his fingers touched me, I'd already become aware he was there—his familiarity, his scent, the tiniest glimpse of his sweater from the corner of my eye.

The point is, you become more attuned to your surroundings and less focussed on mundane things like shopping or lunch. You see more, hear more, understand more. Not everything, of course. But more.

Writing:

A writer often develops a similar open-ness to their surrounds. Not so much looking for potential threats, but just observing more. Looking for stories and people. Reading body language. Listening to interesting (or dull) dialogue. Watching character traits and tics, clothing and appearances; filing them away for future use.

But while martial artists are looking for people who might kill in real life, writers are looking for people to kill off in their stories.

Seeing settings more clearly is important, too. Everywhere a good writer goes, they're often unconsciously (or consciously) taking notes about what buildings, plants, foods, soft furnishings etc look like; what things smell or taste like; what sounds they are hearing; what things feel like underfoot or in their hand.

Craft of Writing Suggestions:

- Go out and people-watch. Don't just listen to dialogue, watch how they move, what they do with their hands, their bodies, their hair, their eyes. Try to work out what they're thinking based on their body language. Anticipate what they'll do next and see if you're right. It's a good way to gain insight into both your characters, and people who might be a threat in the real world.

- Now do some research into how to write that dialogue tightly; how to describe your characters without using clichés like mirrors.

- Then do the same thing with every place you visit. Take photos. Note colours, smells, tastes, shapes, feelings—anything that could be used to add descriptive details or could be used to influence your characters or immerse readers.

- Do an experiment and ask friends/family to glance at a picture or a place, close their eyes and describe what they've seen. What they saw will give you insight into what they think is important—how they filter the world.

An expectant mother might see a baby in a pram but not the dog right beside it. A dog-lover could remember the dog and not the baby. A car enthusiast might remember the vehicle the pram was beside. A single guy may remember the mother was a cute brunette, but might have filtered out the baby completely.

- Now take that concept of filtering and awareness and apply it to each of your characters. What are they interested in and how does that affect how they see the world and describe it?

Part 15—Perseverance

Something to Ponder: When things get hard, do you (or your character) give up or do you persevere? Have you given up learning craft skills because you think you know enough, or you're too busy?

There are weeks when I look at my To Do list and just giggle hysterically, knowing there's no way I can get through it all. The urge is strong to just give up and not bother. If I gave up some things, life would be *so* much easier. But I don't, because my goals are important to me and life is too short to faff about.

Martial Arts:

When we do our hajime classes in aikido, the first one is hard because you don't know what's coming. Those two plus, non-stop, gruelling hours test you deeply. Sometimes the only thing that keeps you going is the fear of looking weak before your sensei and your training partners. Or the sheer bloody-mindedness I mentioned before. The "I will NOT let this beat me" type of thinking.

Many people never come back to the dojo after doing their first hajime.

The second one is even harder because you *do* know what's coming. And you choose to push yourself to the limit again. To persevere when others quit or don't even start. To not give up because you love that rush of self-pride and confidence you get at the end from knowing you've done something really difficult.

Martial arts isn't easy. Training deals painful injuries to body and ego.

But the euphoria of completing a grading, or a first and second hajime class; of being proud of your perseverance and achievement. The rush of endorphins your brain emits when you achieve your goal. That is unbeatable.

Writing:

Often the first book or story you produce is difficult, but you don't really know enough to understand how much harder it could be. So, you grit your teeth and struggle through to the end out of sheer bloody-mindedness.

Or maybe you're one of the lucky ones whose first book just trips off your fingertips like molten gold and fairy dust—easy and fun.

Then you're faced with the second book. Often now accompanied by terrible doubt because (maybe) you've realised how much you didn't know last time. Or maybe you've had a few bad reviews, or sales tanked.

Why do you do it? Why do you persevere and write anyway, even when you might not be getting external validation or monetary rewards?

Biologically, there are a couple of reasons.

1: because humans are addicted to the endorphins our brain releases as a reward for achieving goals. That little glow of pleasure when you type *The End*, or when you hold your actual, printed novel in your hands and smell that heady, papery scent.

That's your brain rewarding you for hard work. It's a neat feedback loop evolution has created to keep you motivated for survival.

Which is why reminding someone of that potential pleasure can be such a strong motivator for them to keep going when times are tough.

Remember the rush.

2: because humans are story-tellers. We are wired to imagine, dream, and tell stories. Sometimes just to ourselves, sometimes to an enthralled audience.

Telling stories is built into our psyche. We were an oral society long before a written one. Story-telling helps to pass on traditions, skills, and memories we treasure.

So never doubt that your urge to produce stories is important to both you and to other people. It's part of being human.

Forget all the doubts and fears that you won't make it. You will.

Persevere. Push through the pain and doubt and exhaustion.

It's worth it to share your vision with the world. Even if you change only one person's life a little bit. Even if all it does is make *you* proud of yourself. It's worth the effort.

Craft of Writing Suggestions:

- If you're not getting positive feedback (or even if you are) now's the time to persevere with learning craft skills. The better you become as a writer, the better your stories will be.

Here are a couple of things to research next.:
- Scene structure—including how to ensure each scene contains a character decision and action that drives the plot naturally to the next scene. (Keep in mind that every time your characters meet an

obstacle, you need to find believable reasons for them to persevere even during the direst circumstance. Their actions have to be consistent with who the character is.)

- How to write a strong opening scene that contains a few key components: the Hook, the Setting, the lead Character, a hint at the Outer Conflict/Plot;

- "Bookending" your story or novel—so it starts and finishes with something symbolic or a matching setting, event, or character. This gives a nice sense of completion to the ending that's satisfying to a reader.

- Embed the key to success in the climax somewhere in the opening scene. This both neatly foreshadows how the protagonist will win, *and* adds depth to the opening scene of the novel.

Part 16—Monkey Mind / No Mind

Something to Ponder: Are you comfortable that it's ok for your first draft to suck? That it's better for your first draft to be simple, rather than over-complicated because you've tried to fit too many things in?

I've spent the last month or so being unable to write anything new. Not because of writer's block, but because of too many competing worries and tasks on my mind.

We all go through times like that. It's not the end of your writing career, but you might need to take a step back and reassess your goals and priorities.

Martial Arts:

There are a couple of useful concepts in martial arts that translate directly to writing and help with this. You may have heard of them.

The first is **Monkey Mind**. It's most frequently referenced in meditation studies. When you're trying so hard to focus on something (breathing, a specific technique, being at peace, repeating something you just did really well) but your mind *will not* settle and focus.

Things pop in: you have to do the shopping on the way home; did the kids do their homework; that horrible person at the office; how very bad you are at (fill in the blank).

When your mind jumps from idea to idea, thought to thought, running and scuttling through your memories, you can't concentrate. Your body won't do what it's supposed to in the dojo. And learning a martial art requires you to consciously train your body to the point where the movements become unconsciously easy.

The point is: It's nigh on impossible to achieve any sort of success while your brain has been hijacked by monkeys on speed.

The second concept is that of **No Mind**. Which is the polar opposite of monkey mind. And hard to achieve without practice. No Mind is when you gain a state of calm emotional distance.

In the beginning, No Mind may be mostly about removing worry and distractions to concentrate on one skill. But as you get better at martial arts—and the body movements become automatic—no mind becomes even more. You release all tension, concentrate on nothing, allow your body to move and your mind to be open to threats—without worry or drowning in fear.

Because fear, overthinking, and worrying all influence your body and brain chemistry, which in turn affect how your body reacts. How fast, how well, how accurately. If you're too focussed on what one guy is going to do, then you're blind to the other guy's actions. Or you second-guess yourself and stuff up the technique.

No Mind is the ideal state when going into a fight. It allows you to act quickly and think logically without being too badly affected by adrenalin and stress.

But it takes practice and experience to kick out the speed-monkeys of distraction and find the sweet spot where fear and adrenalin don't control you.

Writing:

Similarly, with writing, Monkey-Mind is when you have a massive To Do list and are constantly worrying about or remembering tasks, so you get no writing done. Or at least none that you're happy with.

Or maybe your To Do list is an unending outpouring of cool ideas, subplots, characters and craft techniques you think *all* need to be squashed into your first draft.

And perhaps you feel that all of them *must* to be written perfectly, the first time. So you endlessly add, edit and re-edit an incomplete novel as new ideas pop in.

Monkey Mind is a terrible state for writers—or any creatives. When you learn to free your mind from worry and stress, your writing will flow more easily.

No Mind's sense of calm, emotional distance takes practice. But once you sideline the barrage of distracting tasks and new ideas, No Mind allows you to concentrate solely on writing (for example) a first draft simply and quickly.

Then, once your basic first draft is done… that's when you go back and start adding in complexities and depth. That's when you start checking for plot holes and making sure character arcs work. And the third draft is when you start layering even more of those cool ideas and skills in.

Each of those stages will benefit from the clarity allowed by operating in No Mind state, rather than they overwhelming confusion of Monkey Mind.

We all have too much on. Too many things that seem vital. But you'll feel better and achieve more lasting success if you do one thing at a time well, instead of ten things badly.

Life of Writing Suggestions:

- Learn basic meditation to reduce stress in your life and increase creativity. It takes time and patience. But when you can do it, your mind will then be free to concentrate on one thing—your writing—instead of on fifty.

- Try setting aside a dedicated time for writing—free of kids, cleaning, groceries, cooking etc. Free of all the things on your To Do List. The more consistently you do this, the more you'll train your brain to focus on writing during that dedicated time.
  If you're still having trouble focussing, try a few minutes of free-writing to get into the zone before you start your "real" writing for the day.

- Do some physical exercise (yoga, perhaps) to increase blood flow and get the endorphins pumping.

- Research one basic technique to apply at a time. Then go through and systematically apply just that one technique as you're second-drafting. By the time you've done it to two novels, it will be

automatic in your next first draft. Start with this one:
- Active vs Passive writing.

Part 17—Speed, Distance, and Timing

Something to Ponder: How fast do you want your readers to get through your book? And how many books do you want to write per year? Are you writing a slow, leisurely literary masterpiece, or a zippy thriller?

Understanding your genre's expectations will help you pace your story to suit. And will also help you decide how many books you want to produce per year to meet your reader's expectations. These days genre readers expect next-in-series to come out sooner rather than later. But you need to decide what suits your writing style.

Martial Arts:

Speed, distance, and timing are crucial to overcoming an attacker. If you're up against a larger opponent, then their strength is likely to overcome yours—unless you are faster, understand how to manage distances, and can read their movements to get the timing right. It also helps if you can hide your intent—fool your opponent into thinking you'll do one thing, when you actually intend to do another.

All of which can take years of training to master. Too close and your opponent can overwhelm you. Too far and you signal your intent. Too slow and he can counter your technique. And if you mistime the grab or strike altogether, he has the advantage because you've lost the element of surprise, or you're offbalance.

But when you do get it right, there's a sweet moment when it all comes together and your training partner (or opponent) goes sailing through the air and lands with a satisfying thump on the ground. All with minimal effort on your behalf.

Dealing with multiple attackers is a different game again. It's like juggling, with flaming knives, and angry cats.

In spite of what the movies like to show, you can't really deal with 3 people at the exact same time. They won't stand back conveniently waiting while number one hits you. They'll all attack at once.

Which means you need to learn how to line them up, how to move so that only one can come at you at once. Then you can pick them off one at a time until they are all lying about, groaning, on the floor.

It's all about timing, speed, and distance.

Writing:

Your story's pacing, tension, and emotional timing and distance will vary depending on the genre you're writing. Thrillers and other action-based genres will be fast-paced, high tension, but often with greater emotional distance. So the reader is swept along by the galloping plot, excited to see if the hero/ine can save the world. But they might not be emotionally caught up and are unlikely to be heartbroken if a character dies.

A romance or family drama might have a slower pace with more emphasis on close, intimate awareness of the hero/ine's inner thoughts and feelings. Reader-tears are more common in this type of story. And a crime novel might focus on deception, red herrings and distraction to fool the reader so they can't guess who the killer is.

But, with any of them, when you get the pacing, tension, emotional distance, and timing right, there's a pay off for the reader. They are invested in knowing how it turns out. Dragged along to the end by the excitement of the external plot, or the pathos of the internal conflict. There should be a moment in the climax scene when they go "Ahhhh! I should have seen that coming. All the clues were there! Wow. That was so cleverly done."

That's when you know you've succeeded in mastering pace, tension, plot event timing, and the reader's emotional distance.

If you decide to write multiple books in a year—or you're working on several in a series at the same time—you need to learn to juggle those flaming knives and angry cats.

It can be difficult to keep your plots and characters distinct if you're constantly shifting between one story and another. They can get mixed up and you can end up with characters invading each other's stories (not really, but they can sound alike).

Then there's the issue of quality. Many authors who produce a lot of books quickly sacrifice the 'resting' time for their novels. If possible, try to allow a couple of months (at least). Put your story aside and DO NOT read it.

Then, when you come back, you see the story with fresh eyes and less emotion. You find plot holes and glaring character issues you missed because you were too close to the story before.

This emotional distance is vital to producing the best possible manuscript.

But these days speed of release helps to secure loyal readers. And timing a release to co-incide with certain holidays, school breaks, movie releases etc could make or break your book's visibility and marketing success. I have one acquaintance whose book took 8 years to go from acceptance by a major publisher to actually being in print. Unfortunately, that's too long a wait. Readers have found new favourite authors by then.

Business of Writing Suggestions:

- Start researching how long it will take your chosen publisher to release your book.

- Chat with small press publishers and compare their release times with larger publishers

- Chat with Indie authors and have a similar discussion.

Craft of Writing Suggestions:

- Research Story pacing and tension—how, when, and why to write fast scenes vs slower scenes.

- Formatting paragraphs, chapters, and sentences to influence story pacing and tension.

- How to handle cliffhangers (hint—readers hate them, in general)

- Dramatic Irony—Increasing tension by giving the reader information the protagonist doesn't have

Part 18—Power

Something to Ponder: How deliberate are you being in your writing? How powerful? How subtle? How *interesting*?

This week in my writing I've been angsting...trying to understand how to write powerfully, so I can pull the reader along and make them feel what I want them to feel. It's not easy. (For me, anyway. I'm quite pragmatic.)

Martial Arts:

When you first begin, your throws have no power and are quite predictable because you only know one or two. Quite frankly, you're crap and your partner is doing all the work. You're doing well to move your foot to the right place. It's physically impossible to master the subtleties because you haven't yet mastered the gross movements.

Every movement is bigger than it needs to be. Every punch is obvious to your partner. You're just going through the motions, copying what the blackbelts do as best you can, not understanding how to move people.

If someone attacked you a few weeks after your first martial arts lesson—or perhaps even a year after—you'd probably revert to basic instinct and flail wildly at them. If you did manage a throw or a lock or a punch, it wouldn't be as strong and centred as someone who had been training for years.

And that's *fine*. As long as you continue to train past that point.

But many people—especially those who are physically strong—never look for the subtle ways the human body can be manipulated. They remain focussed on the gross and middle-level movements. Those requiring strength rather than power.

But the more you practice, the more you understand the difference between strength and power. And as you master the nuances of the art, your techniques become powerful and effortless and unpredictable. Your art will become uniquely yours, in subtle ways.

And it's the subtleties that make it powerful. How you shift your weight. The angle of your wrist or foot. Where your centre of balance lies.

Finally, your training partner *must* go with your throw or risk a broken or dislocated arm.

Mastering those subtle aspects of the art allows you to surprise, shock, and move people against their expectations. Without using strength to bludgeon them into submission.

Writing:

As a writer, most of us begin by writing derivatively; bluntly. Rehashing things we loved as a reader. We write obvious, predictable plotlines and shallow characters in obvious, predictable ways, not realising they've been done to death.

We'll often hit people over the head with preachy themes. Or have no theme at all, so the work seems flat and has no power to resonate. We're spilling fairly ordinary words without understanding how to move the reader's heart. Or how to write powerfully.

Then you learn the things you didn't know about. Story structure and how to use that to build tension. How to interweave theme and character arcs to help readers relate to characters. Or you start to understand tropes and how to subvert expectations in unpredictable ways that both surprise and delight jaded readers.

Once you get your head around these large-scale ideas, then you start to work on scene-level and sentence-level techniques. How to create tension within the scene, between characters, or with setting. How to set mood with word choices. How to make the reader want to keep reading past the end of the chapter. How to write in ways that resonate with the reader and immerse them in the breathtaking wonder of your make-believe world.

How to write powerfully, subtly, and beautifully—in your own voice.

But it's a work in progress. Forever, as far as I can tell. And it follows the law of diminishing returns—a steep learning curve to start with. Then it flattens out and you learn in tiny increments until you feel like you're getting nowhere.

It's only when you look back to the very beginning that you realise how far your writing has come.

But that's what learning is about. No-one's perfect to begin with. But everyone can be powerful, if they are willing to work at it.

And it's the subtleties of your writing—how you manipulate words, images, and feelings—that lends power to your stories and allows you to surprise, shock, and move people.

Craft of Writing Suggestions:

- Analyse your work looking for issues you'd like to refine and improve. Spend time researching and working on them.

- If you feel your story isn't powerful enough, consider how you could make it different from others in the same genre. What can you add that's new, deeply emotional, or just surprising?

- Practice brainstorming how to subvert common plots and tropes

- Use strange/unusual settings, characters, and plot twists.

- Research how not to Infodump on your reader— how to drip-feed vital information.

- Research Foreshadowing

- Research how to add Red herrings to mystery, crime, thriller, suspense stories etc

Part 19—Breath Control

Something to Ponder: How often do you just stop, close your eyes, and breathe to centre yourself?

Haven't written one of these modules in a while. Life got a little crazy. I forgot to stop and just be; just breathe. We all live insanely busy lives. Apparently busy is the new black. It's easy to forget to centre yourself.

Martial Arts:

In Aikido one of the key concepts is breath control. Breathing in to prepare for a throw or lock. Breathing out when you throw someone or put a lock on. Regulating the flow of breath so you're not gasping for air because of exertion and adrenalin.

Some branches of Aikido talk about the 'spiritual' element to the exhalation and its connection to power, but there are more practical reasons for mastering breath control.

1: Your brain analyses the scent of the air and uses it to judge danger. The smell of a wild animal; the smell of fear sweat; the smell of off meat. All warning signals that can trigger a fear-response in you.

That causes a cascade of chemicals in your blood preparing you for fight/flight/freeze type reactions. Your reasoning mind goes a bit haywire and you become terrible at making smart, cool decisions.

But if the stress is purely in your mind—your own anxieties, not any physical danger—then taking slow, deep breaths helps convince your mind there's no actual threat. So it can help to calm you.

That's why meditation teaches so much on breathing. It gives you something to focus on to distract you from the quicksand of fear and anxiety.

2: Breathing out—whether accompanied by a strong 'ki-ai' cry or just a sharp breath—does help to focus your power when you're throwing or locking someone up. A loud 'ki-ai' can also terrify and momentarily distract an attacker. (Or your unruly children, perhaps?)

Breathing and recognising how breath can affect your thinking and emotions is essential in martial arts.

Actually, it should be essential in everything.

Writing:

You'll often be faced with roadblocks. Either an overwhelming amount of stuff to do to achieve your writing career goals, or perhaps writers block, or kids taking up your time and energy, or the stress of trying to understand and interact successfully with people.

Sometimes it's just that you've written your characters into a corner and don't know how to get them out. Or you've half-finished a novel and can't see how to get to the end. Or you hate everything you've written and don't know how to make it better.

In pretty much every instance, if you step away and take a few long, deep breaths, you'll find yourself calming down.

Next time you're stressed about a story going wrong, or a bad review, or some apparently insurmountable problem.... just take a few slow breaths in and let them out. Relax your shoulders and jaw. Feel the breath go right down into your body's centre. Release it on a scream if you need to. Or just let the stress go as much as you can with each breath.

Your brain will "taste" the air and understand there's no external threat and the stress hormones will start to reduce in your blood and brain.

Try it.

Craft of Writing Suggestions:

- Go research a couple of new craft techniques. Take a deep breath to fortify yourself, then try applying the new techniques to your messy first draft to improve the prose. That will help you feel better about your writing.

- Here are three to try out:
    - How and when to Show rather than Telling.
    - How and when to Tell rather than Showing
    - How and when to write flashbacks into a story

Part 20—Self Control

Something to Ponder*:* How good are you at recognising and managing your emotional reactions?

I was in the shopping centre a few months ago and watched a toddler throw the biggest tantrum. It was epic. The parent dealt with it quite calmly, leaving the child to scream and informing her that when she could control herself, the parent would listen. I almost applauded.

Self-control is slightly different to self-discipline (which we covered earlier). To my mind, self-control is more about knowing when certain emotions are appropriate to reveal, and when they are best off sent to their rooms to sulk. When they will do good and when they will do harm.

Martial Arts:

In aikido, the most frequent, potentially-damaging emotion seen is frustration. Usually it's self-directed. People can't make their bodies do what they "should".

Or they can't see how the instructor is making a technique work.

The student's first temptation is usually to muscle their way through. To descend into anger and frustration at being thwarted and react like a child having a tantrum by doing the technique harder and faster.

Or the opposite happens. People give in to self-doubt, throw up their hands and say "I can't do it. It's too hard."

When people are eager beginners, they usually put aside their feelings of inadequacy and decide to learn (if they don't quit). But when you're a higher belt and learning the nuances of a technique, it can be a real blow to the ego to suddenly realise you've been doing it not-quite-right the whole time.

If you train with a higher-belt partner who resists in order to teach you something new, that's the money moment.

It takes a great deal of self-awareness to put aside the urge to bull through—or the urge to ignore their advice. It takes self-control to put aside the resentment and self-doubt, and to open up to re-learning what you thought you already knew. To accept critique when you just want to hear that you are perfect, already.

It's not easy, but if you control your automatic, first-reaction emotions and let them slide, you find deeper ones you can explore—buried beliefs and emotions that, once analysed and released, will free you up to absorb helpful advice without feeling threatened or frustrated.

There's nothing quite like the rush of endorphins when you put aside emotion, learn the next step, and your training partner collapses in a heap with a faint scream of surprise.

Writing

As a writer (or a martial artist), there's nothing wrong with frustration—as long as you don't give up or let it cloud your ability to make clear decisions. Harnessed properly, and controlled, frustration can be an excellent impetus to get it right.

If your writing mentor decides that you're now ready for deeper critiquing, you have a choice of reactions. When your story comes back covered in red marks, crossed out words, and a margin full of comments, you can either suck it up and decide to learn, or you can ignore the advice because it hurts to hear you aren't perfect.

Up to you.

If you do study and absorb their ideas, that writing breakthrough moment when you finally get it…that's the best. Those 'ah-ha' revelations when you understand how to shade your writing with a specific nuance or tone, or how to show a character's emotion, or how to tie up three loose ends in one scene...those are fabulous.

Because that's often followed by a reader contacting you and saying 'OMG, that just blew me away.'

And that's pure gold.

Learn self-control of your emotions so you can open yourself up to new skills and new levels of brilliance.

Craft of Writing Suggestions:

- Research how to manipulate your reader's emotions vs how to show your character's emotions. They are two different things, both equally important.

- Research how to *show* your character's emotions with their dialogue, facial expressions, actions, and body language—rather than just *telling* the reader how the character feels.

- Research how to "layer" your character's emotions realistically when they react/respond to some event.

- Research Filter Words and how they can be removed to bring the reader closer to the character's emotions, or included to increase the distance between the reader and the character's feelings.

- Know what mood and tone you want to set for each scene and choose the right words to suit.

- Keep in mind that best-selling books tend to be ones that let the reader into the characters' minds and hearts. I don't mean just romantically, I mean all emotions. Show the reader how your character is feeling. When you're plotting out scenes and actions, make sure to include a note about how the character feels at that moment; how they react to what happens; how that emotion affects their next decision.

Part 21—Never be the Best

Something to Ponder: Do you (or your characters) spend too much time hiding in your comfort zone, protecting yourself?

Comfort zones. We all want to be in one. They're comfortable, by definition. But they're not where we learn new skills or where we do our best work. They're not where we find out who we really are.

(They are good places to recuperate after undergoing the stress of change, however, so don't chuck them out altogether.)

Martial Arts:

You most often find people wallowing in their comfort zone once they hit their first blackbelt. Whitebelts look at you with a bit of hero-worship. You often get asked to be uke (partner) for your sensei when he demonstrates (which is considered a mark of your ability as an uke). You're called on to help lower belts learn new techniques. It can be a heady time. So it's easy to feel like you've made it and you can cruise now.

Which, if your sensei is keeping an eye on you, is normally when he/she steps in and demonstrates something you don't understand. Or points out a flaw in a technique you thought you had down pat.

How do you react? Do you suck up your pride and hurl yourself out of your comfort zone again? Back into the world of uncertainty and frustration you spent so long pulling yourself out of?

Or do you ignore the promptings and rest on the laurels already achieved; bask in the warm fuzzies that come from passing on knowledge to new students.

Don't get me wrong. There's absolutely nothing wrong with passing on knowledge and enjoying helping others. You learn a lot from teaching people, as well. I quite enjoy it, myself.

But there's a danger in it, too. A danger of becoming too comfortable and too used to adulation. A danger of believing your own publicity, as they say. A danger of thinking you know everything, or even enough and don't need any more help.

Writing:

The same happens in the writing world. Writers who have a few acceptances under their belts, maybe a

Creative Writing degree, or a few awards, a few published books. They gather a group of acolytes and mentor them along the path. It feels good. Everyone likes to be listened to and respected.

It's a comfortable place to sit. No-one is telling you you're not good enough, because you're top of your little pyramid.

And you do, undoubtedly, learn from teaching and analysing other people's writing.

But there comes a time when you have to push yourself again. There are always new things to learn. Always new ideas, new craft techniques, new ways of seeing the world, or how stories work. And these days the publishing industry changes so fast (as does reader taste) that you can't afford to sit back and gloat over how great a writer you are.

There's always someone who knows something you don't. Never arrogantly believe that you are the only one with good ideas and experience.

Find people better than you. Make yourself uncomfortably uncertain again.

It takes humbleness, determination, and a dollop of self-awareness to push through the boundary between the comfort zone and the discomfort zone.

But it's worth it for how much better you become, and how much larger your new comfort zone is when you master the new skills.

The best blackbelts, and the best writers, are (I find, anyway) the ones who are most humble, least self-aggrandizing, and most open to learning from anyone.

Craft of Writing Suggestions:

- Research how to self-edit. Get used to ruthlessly killing off your favourite phrases, characters, words and scenes.

- Start looking for flaws in your writing and keep a list of your common mistakes and your overused words. Use it to self-edit your next story.

- Research the following, for starters (because what you learned in High School is not the whole story—pun intended):
    - How to use Past tenses vs Present tenses vs Future tenses.
    - Correct grammar, punctuation and spelling

Part 22—Simplifying

Something to Ponder: Does your story and style suit the reader and the genre?

I recently wrote an extremely complex tapestry novel and loved it. So many interwoven characters and plots, I needed a massive spreadsheet to keep track of everything. I learned a heap about how to write unique and distinctive character voices.

But was it the right style for the genre I wrote in? Should it have been simpler? Although it has worked well, I'm sure there are some readers who will find it too complicated and toss it aside for an easier-read. Does that matter?

Not to me, because I wrote it in order to teach myself one, specific skill.

But it might to you, if you are writing for income and a big readership.

So when do you simplify and why?

Martial Arts.

In any combat situation, simpler techniques will generally work better than tricky, complicated ones. When you're under stress and/or panicking, large parts of your higher brain function shut down and the old 'fight-flight-freeze' responses kick in. They are so primitive that you lose about 70% of your fine motor skills and resort to gross motor skills—random arm-waving, wild punches, screaming/flailing.

That's why dojos spend so much time doing mock-combat simulation and gradings. The sensei is attempting to reproduce the surge of adrenalin and fear you get in a real fight.

Of course it's not quite the same, but a dojo-trained martial artist may handle a stressful situation better than someone with no training at all.

But every trained, experienced martial artist and combat experienced person will tell you the same thing: Don't try anything finicky and complex when you're under the adrenalin dump rush.

Keep it simple. Keep it short. Keep it sharp and to the point.

Writing:

When self-editing, it's worth keeping that same advice in mind.

It does depend, somewhat, on your genre. If you're writing lyrical, poetic, literary "prose" (often with little external plot, but with a lot of lovely, complex sentences and beautiful words) then keeping things simple and to the point is *not* what you're going for.

But if you're writing genre fiction, the modern "rules" are aimed at removing such "purple prose" in favour of shorter sentences and plainer language. Because that's what many time-poor modern readers are used to.

So look at simplifying your stories if it suits your market of readers. Shorter, sharper scenes; shorter sentences, less complicated words, fewer characters and fewer tricky subplots—all these allow for faster reading.

In novels you can often combine scenes and reduce characters to tighten the narrative and increase pacing and tension. Simplify sentences in faster scenes, make them more complex in slower scenes. Use clear themes that are universal and appeal to all humans.

Tighten your plots and subplots so they are closely interwoven with your theme and character growth rather than wandering off on sidetracks unconnected with the main plot. Keep things neat and clean (depending on your genre).

Craft of Writing Suggestions:

- Read different genres and note which ones use high-action/fast-paced scenes (eg: Thrillers) with minimal time spent on character emotional responses afterward. Then compare to other genres (eg: Romances or women's fiction) which often uses simpler, shorter action scenes, followed by slower emotion-focussed sections.

- Cut out and combine characters, excess subplots, and scenes to tighten narrative.

- Cut out unnecessary character actions / movements.

- Research the difference between Action Beats and Dialogue Tags and learn when each are useful and when they can be culled.

- Find your often-repeated "weasel" or "crutch" words. Make a list and delete a large percentage or substitute alternatives for variety.

- Research how to correct "overwriting".

- Remove unneeded words and unneeded modifiers that slow things down

- Research "microtiming" and how to fix it for reader clarity and smooth reading.

- Correct unclear modifiers.

- Learn how to remove/replace slower verbs with faster ones.

- Remove action-slowing words like "suddenly" and "a moment later".

Part 23—Prioritising

Something to Ponder: How much time do you *really* spend writing?

Life has a habit of interfering with our creative passions. Work gets in the way of writing, family gets in the way, even cleaning gets in the way.

But it's funny how a life-threatening situation focuses your priorities like nothing else.

Martial Arts:

As a martial artist, one of the most crucial things you must do is decide your priorities. Both *before* you ever get into a threatening situation, and *while* you're in it.

These are two different mindsets.

Before you're bailed up by a badguy, you need to know what you're prepared to do—how far you'll go to protect yourself or your loved ones. Will you only twist arms, or will you break them? What is your priority—survival or not doing serious damage?

The two may be incompatible.

If you haven't thought about your limits and what's most important to you, in advance, you'll hesitate and lose the chance to choose.

During a confrontation, you need to also prioritise what actions will get you the optimal outcome. Running away is great. Failing that, talking your way out is good. Failing that, doing minimum damage in order to escape is important for both legal and psychological reasons. Your last choice should (in our society) be causing serious injury or death.

But again, if you haven't trained in understanding how to assess the situation and prioritise each choice, you'll fail to do so under stress and default to something useless or terrible.

Writing:

The problem with writing (or anything creative) is that it's highly unlikely to be something you prioritise due to a sudden, life-threatening situation. Pen and sword metaphors aside.

We focus on the mundane parts of our lives over the creative ones because the mundane is (at its basic level) about survival. If we don't earn an income, we don't eat and eating equates to survival. If we don't care for our offspring they don't survive, and we are genetically programmed to reproduce and nurture.

Which means we prioritise eating and care for offspring over pretty much everything else. And we view our lives as being fuzzily endless with an unlimited number of "one days" during which there will magically be time to do the creative stuff our brains love.

As writers, we need to find the balance; decide what our priorities truly are. Otherwise life becomes so much about caring for family and putting food on the table that we never get around to filling that black hole in our gut with the creativity light.

Until it's too late.

Life of Writing Suggestions:

- Think Ahead. Stop for a second an imagine you've just been told you have sharply limited time left. You now have to truly prioritise what you are passionate about.

   If it's writing, then decide exactly what you want to say. And put it on the top of your To Do list for once. Other stuff can wait and you probably won't even notice if it's not all done and perfect.

   So what if the bathroom isn't spotless, or your kids go to bed a bit late? Who cares if their clothes aren't ironed or they eat nothing but hotdogs and mac and cheese for a couple of days while you finish the story? They'll survive, I promise. They might even learn to cook and clean.

- Think now about what legacy you want to leave behind. Family, yes, but you have something to say as well. Don't leave it too late to prioritise what makes you unique to the world. What's inside your head.

  Your gift. Your words. Your voice.

Part 24—Passing on Knowledge

Something to Ponder: Are you hoarding information, or can you pass it on to help other writers?

As I said at the beginning, I'm far from an expert in writing. I still have a lot to learn and I feel somewhat arrogant even writing this How To.

But circumstances have forced my hand.

Which made me realise that passing on knowledge is also a survival skill. On an evolutionary level it helps our offspring to survive, and on a personal level it helps us to survive.

How? We're a troupe/tribal animal. We need other humans to help us survive on a physical level. The more people who know the important information about hunting, gathering, making fire etc, the more of our troupe (including us) are likely to live.

But we also need to feel valued, respected, even admired. Because that ensures us a place by the fire, food to eat, comfort and succor when we're unwell. Being a font of wisdom helps us gain that respect and in turn gives us all the "feels" (those reward-endorphins mentioned earlier).

Our mental health is (at least a bit) dependent on being accepted, admired, respected in our troupe and in our family.

But it's a double-edged sword.

We've all met people who know a little and come across like they know it all—we lose respect for them when their lack of skill shows through.

When, exactly, are we qualified to pass on our knowledge? When do we know enough to make sharing valid?

Martial Arts:

In the dojo we see this a lot. White belts, having newly learnt how to twist people into human origami, are eager to share with anyone who is dumb enough to put their hand out. Even brown belts tell everyone they are a brown belt and excitedly demonstrate the latest skills.

But in a good dojo, you'll find the higher the blackbelt, the less likely they are to tell you what their belt colour is or demonstrate without good reason. They don't need anyone's validation. And they often won't push knowledge onto a brownbelt or above unless the student specifically asks for help.

I still remember when my Sensei handed over my shiny new blackbelt, embroidered with my name in kanji. He bowed and said with a wry smile, *"Now you can begin to learn."*

And I understood what he meant. I felt humbled by the sheer weight of what I *didn't* know. The subtlety of the art I still didn't understand. The skill of the higher belts. Their willingness to both help and let me learn for myself.

I also recall a blackbelt who, after doing something unacceptably arrogant, was stripped of his belt. He had the choice of leaving the dojo or starting all over again.

I respect deeply that he started again. Re-did every grading until he got back to blackbelt. It took him two years. He became a much better person. Shut up more. Put aside his ego.

His character, knowledge, and skill were proven beyond a doubt.

Writing:

In writing it's a lot harder to tell who you should respect; who is worth listening to. Anyone can put up a website and call themselves a "best-selling author", or an "editor". Anyone can claim they have a creative writing degree. As a new author it's easy to get overwhelmed by the volume of advice—some conflicting, some useful.

It's also easy to get sucked into the desire to pass on what you've learned to someone who might be just a couple of steps behind you.

That's whitebelt thinking.

A good rule of thumb is *Ask don't Tell*. Ask them what they already know, then ask what they want to know. Then resist the urge to tell and, instead, point them in the right direction to gain that knowledge.

There may be places they can learn that are more experienced and with more complete information. For example: Editors registered with a valid organisation and with qualifications and experience. Authors with multiple awards and mega-best-selling books (but not just #1 on a niche Amazon category in a small country). Entire Writers Centres; specialist trainers giving high-quality workshops. Writers Conferences all over the world.

You don't need your ego validated. Focus your time on learning more, on improving your own writing. Try to refrain from teaching others until you're at least a brown belt—until you have a couple of well-respected novels or short story collections out there in the world. Until you are certain you have the skills to engage and excite readers.

I'm only saying this because I made this mistake, myself. Tried to help others—very well-meaning, as we all are—earlier than I should have. We've all muddled along ok, but I could have done better. Definitely could have shut up more.

Like martial arts, writing should not be about ego and having people look up to you. For me, personally, both are about doing something you're passionate about; becoming a stronger, better person; living a richer, fuller life.

Then, when you're skilled in your art… that's when you pass on what you know to those who want to hear it.

It might not be that way for you, of course. Your choice.

But for me, writing is not about gaining admiration. It's about learning and growing and turning that experience into stories about life. Stories that help others learn about themselves and about how to be better people.

Craft of Writing Suggestions:

- Seek out mentors—people whose writing and humility you respect and admire. Ask if they'll help you learn. Be prepared to pay for their expertise. It will be worth it.

- Research more subtle ways of improving your writing and practice them. These will gain you recognition as an excellent writer—if that's what you're after. Here's a few I got handed by my mentor. Feel free to look them up if they sound useful:
    - Metaphors & similes—don't overuse them, though. Create beautiful, unique, new ones that make your reader sigh in delight at the image they create.
    - Symbols & symbolism—these can be powerful and subtle when tied to your theme and character arcs
    - Poetic devices—there are so many to choose from and they can lend beauty and rhythm to your prose

- Here's a few other easier things to try
    - Remove/replace any boring verbs and adjectives and replace with stronger ones
    - Remove lots of your overworked adverbs and find stronger verbs to use, instead
    - Be specific and interesting in your setting description words and choose only those relevant to character, plot, or theme.

- Be careful and deliberate with your word choices—bear in mind how words affect emotions and create vivid mental images
- Use descriptions featuring all 5 senses (taste, smell, touch, sound, sight) to immerse the reader in the scene.
- When your story is done and fully edited to the best of your ability, read it aloud (or use a read-aloud function if your software has it). That will help pick up any awkward sentences or duplicate words.

Part 25—Facing Darkness—Mental Health

Something to Ponder: How high are your expectations for yourself? Are they realistic? Are you beating yourself up when your human and make mistakes?

I don't claim to be an expert in mental health by any means. Nor am I saying mental health issues can be solved by *deciding* to be OK. I wish it were that simple. All I can give you is my perspective on the things that have affected me over the years and hope it helps you in some way.

These last couple of months have been... challenging.

But the challenges have made me think about what I've learned over the years from doing martial arts and from writing, and from all the other things I've done through my life.

I was raised on the old mindset that being perfect/excellent at something the first time you try equates to being valuable/lovable. It comes from when adults praise kids for their birth-traits (beauty, speed, strength, intelligence etc) rather than their learned traits (determination, focus, hard work, willingness to fail and learn). Or adults who constantly criticise kids for *not* being perfect the first time.

My self-worth came from being good at things. Which creates a nasty self-esteem loop. If you're not good the first time, then you're a failure and not lovable.

(NOTE: I recommend a book called *Mindset* by Dr Carol S Dweck to understand how this affects you and your kids)

But, because I have a genius-level older brother to compare myself to, I also had to work my arse off to *be* good at anything.

And that determination to work hard and be excellent builds over time and becomes habit. It makes the next skill you try easier because you've already learned that failure is part of the deal. You've learned to control your body, or your mind in order to succeed.

I just didn't realise that's what I was doing, until much later in life.

Martial Arts:

In the dojo, we get a *lot* of people who start and think they will be instinctively brilliant at martial arts. And sometimes they are—to a point. But there is *always* a moment (in any skill) where you hit a wall. Where your natural gifts are no longer enough for things to come easily. Where you must fail, learn, and work hard in order to improve.

That's the point where most people raised in the wrong mindset give up. And all the excuses come out.

They're tired. Martial arts hurts. They have to work late. The traffic was too heavy and they couldn't get to class. Someone in the dojo wasn't nice to them. Someone senior in the dojo told them what to do and they didn't want to do it.

You hear them all.

But really, it often boils down to insecurity. A fear that you weren't good enough the first time you tried, therefore you're inherently flawed and will never be good enough.

Which leads to anxiety. What do people think of me?

If we could take anxiety about what other people think away from humans, the world would be a vastly better place.

There would be no need for the dominance games that go with tribal/troupe living. No need for the constant belittling of others in an attempt to make yourself feel better. None of the nagging twist in the guts, the whisper in your ear, the checking to see how others are responding.

Returning to the dojo after failure. Attempting a technique again when you did it wrong the first time. Coming back to the dojo after you're bruised, exhausted, in tears, and feeling like you'll never get it right.

That's where the toughness comes in. That's where the mindset and mental health and self-belief begins.

Writing:

Writing is no different. You write and put your work out there. If you're intending to make a career of writing, you'll do some learning and test the waters with beta readers and editors before you publish, but many people don't. And in this age of self-publishing, that means you can receive some nasty trolling from people who are horribly insecure and desperate to pull others down.

(Pro tip: try not to read reviews if you can help it. No matter how good they are, you'll get upset or depressed over some comment someone made. If you *must* read them, just remember: what people say about you is mostly a mirror of their own insecurities and fears.)

This is where mindset makes a huge difference. Every time you fuck up (or someone says you have), it's an opportunity to learn, to accept that you're not perfect—*and* to accept that it's OK to not be perfect. You'll never please everyone. Nor should you try.

It's really easy to hide at home and attempt to avoid the trolls, the negativity, the potential of failure.

But every time you get out of the house, go to a workshop to learn how to be a better writer; put pen back to paper again in spite of criticism… *that's* where mental toughness and mental health is.

And it builds. It gets easier.

Once you've done it a few times, your brain knows you can pick yourself up after failure; knows you can try again, because you've done it before. The neural pathways exist now. And the more you use those pathways—by trying again, ignoring the trolls, writing anyway, learning more—the easier those pathways become to tread.

Until the pathways of mental toughness become wider and stronger than the ones of anxiety and fear.

Anything worth doing will only come with failure and learning. You just have to choose the right path each time to get to the destination you really want.

But it takes time. And effort.

And which path to take is a decision. Your decision. Every time.

Not an easy one. Believe me, I know.
And it's ok to ask for help.

Life of Writing Suggestion:

- If you took my earlier suggestion and joined a writers group, reach out to people in it when you're doing it tough. I guarantee they are as well. Go for coffee. Talk about what you're trying to achieve. *Listen* as well—friendships are not one-sided.

  Rekindle your joy in writing and belief in yourself by understanding that you're not alone; you're not the only one feeling inadequate; you're not the only one afraid to put yourself out there for fear of getting stomped on. But you can support and encourage each other.

  And, as a group, you can all get through the tough times if you reach out and *talk, listen, encourage,* and *never criticise*. Even if you mean well.

- Never criticise.

- Never criticise.

- I'll say it again… never criticise the work of a fellow writer in your writers group.

- *Critique* your fellow writers' work, by all means—if they ask you to. But understand the difference between critiquing and criticising.

Critiquing is analysing their story in a logical way to find both the pros and cons. Then pointing out—constructively—*both* the good aspects of their writing and the parts that need work (in your opinion). Even if you hate their story, find something about it—their words, their effort, their perseverance, their enthusiasm…whatever. Find something admirable and tell them. And they can accept well-meaning constructive advice on the story's flaws more easily if it's sandwiched between honest, positive feedback.

Then watch them blossom and grow. People gain confidence if they are honestly praised for their work and learning (not their birth-traits).

Part 26—Writing THE END—Facing Death

Something to Ponder: We take our lives, loved ones and available time too much for granted.

When I was younger, I experienced a couple of instances where I was genuinely worried that I might be either killed or violently injured. That was, in fact, a large reason why I took up martial arts.

Now, unfortunately, I'm staring down the barrel of a potentially slower death. I've recently been diagnosed with metastatic melanoma/cancer. Yes, we've tried all the options and nothing has worked beyond buying a couple of extra months.

Hence this is the final post in this series. But hopefully it's helped you find some new skills and confidence in your chosen form of madness—writing.

Martial Arts:

Martial arts often has an underlying ethos around confronting potential death with grace and honour. Which is easy when you're on the mat, but harder when it's reality.

When you're faced with sudden death, there's not a lot of time to think. It all happens too fast. How you handle it physically and mentally is related to your past experiences and training. You just…react and try to survive in that short, sharp, painful moment. Then, afterward, you deal with the fallout of post traumatic stress etc.

If you're wise, you take your survival and run with it—absorb the wake-up call and stop fucking about with your life; start to *do* the things on your bucket list before it's too late.

When you're presented with the uncertainty of a potentially lingering death, there's too much time to think. And no clear deadline.

You start to regret the things you never had a chance to do; or worry about how your loved ones will cope without you; or wish you could help to make it easier for family and friends.

Then there's the problem of Denial—which makes it hard to believe your plans for the future won't happen. Death isn't in your face this exact minute, and who wants to believe it, anyway? It's also difficult to do anything when it feels ultimately pointless.

You need to stop what you're doing right now—*before* you're faced with the prospect of either a sudden or lingering end—and make some decisions about how you'll manage life and handle death.

Writing:

If you are sitting there, not writing (or not doing anything you have on your wish-list) because you're afraid of what people will say or whether your work will be recognised/successful, then remember:

If you die without ever writing what you need to say, the world is a worse place because of it.

If your words help just one person get through a tough day, then they were worth writing.

If your story helps one lonely child or dying adult to feel understood, then get your pen out, now.

Don't let fear of people stop you from contributing.

Don't let fear of "career-death" stop you from sharing yourself with the world. Your career won't end/die if you make a mistake or write one truly terrible story.

The only way to end your dream is to stop writing.

You won't ever regret being more, but you will regret not trying to be.

And, one day, when you are gone... your words and thoughts might be the only slivers of you left for your family and friends to cling to and treasure.

Dying is difficult, messy and painful. But dying without living, first, is even worse.

Life of Writing Suggestions:

- Mortality gives meaning to life. Use that knowledge wisely. Get off your arse and do things. Learn new skills. Help people make the most of their lives.

- Hug people more often. Tell everyone you care about exactly what is special about them. Don't be stingy with your love and your praise. You don't know how long they'll be around.

- Write, submit, suck up the rejections, write more, learn more, submit more. Rinse and repeat.

- Learn how people think and create characters who think differently from you. Then learn from them.

- Be the person, the parent, the lover, the friend, the writer, that you've always wanted to be.

- Be kind. Be generous. Be more than you thought you could.

When you write THE END on your story, or your life, know that you gave it your best shot; lived and died with grace and honour that would make your sensei, your friends, and your family proud of you—and you proud of yourself.

Hopefully this has helped you. And hopefully I'll meet you in Valhalla and we can share a drink, sing a song, and wave a sword around together.

#

END

About the Author: Aiki Flinthart

This is not meant to be braggy or make anyone feel bad. I just thought I'd make a list of all the things I've done in my life. This is how I chose to live my life, but it's not necessarily for everyone. Mostly this list is for my son and husband. But who knows, this list might inspire someone reading this book to go out and try a few weird and wonderful activities.

NOTE: I'm not from a wealthy family. I was raised by a single mother who loved outdoor activities and sports. We owned very little in the way of "things", but she counted and saved every cent so my brother and I could try new experiences and discover what we loved to do.

I am deeply grateful for that, because she passed on to me an awareness of how to manage money so I could buy experiences rather than things, a love of learning, and a determination to overcome my fears—all of which stood me in good stead.

Some of the below-listed I've only done a couple times, for fun. Some I stuck with to the point where I mastered the skill. Some as a kid, or teenager. Some as a young adult or adult. Some on my own. Some with family and friends.

All are memories I treasure.

I regret nothing.

NOTE: in case anyone is wondering, I'm an introvert, so I'm not big on spending lots of time with lots of people. I need time on my own to recharge and recuperate. Which is partly why I love writing so much. But I'm also a bit of an adrenalin junkie—hence all the action-heavy hobbies and sports on this list.

- Swam in freshwater creeks and slid down waterfalls
- Swung from trees and dropped into lakes
- Body surfing at beaches
- Bareback and saddled horseriding
- Ten-pin bowling, roller skating, tennis, and golf (the first two quite well, the last two quite badly)
- Reef-snorkelled and deep-water ocean-fished (got very seasick)
- Swam with dolphins
- Traipsed through mangroves and forests
- Hiked up mountains and through rainforests
- Learned to drive a 4WD out 'bush' safely.
- Rock climbing and abseiling

- Competitive swimming, basketball, softball, and vigaro – to state level
- Whitewater rafting and liloing down rivers
- Windsurfing
- SCUBA diving licence + sailed on maxi yacht (got very seasick)
- Waterskiing, barefoot skiing, and skiboat driver's licence
- Learned the basics of sign language
- Snow-skiing, snow-sledding, ice skating on frozen lakes
- Go-karting (almost matched the amateur driver's course record)
- Pistol shooting, rifle shooting, skeet shooting
- Skydiving and bunji jumping
- Spelunking and fossil hunting
- Hiking and helicoptering over a glacier
- Starwatching, and observing the moon eclipse while lying on a beach at night.
- Camping, birdwatching, feeding possums, roasting potatoes in the campfire coals, roasting marshmallows
- Swimming in deep, freezing mountain lakes
- A geology degree, with Honours focussed on vulcanology

- Field assistant for marine geologist in the Whitsunday Islands (got very seasick)
- Hiking on fresh volcanic lava (my shoes melted) and observing flowing lava through a lava tube window on Hawaii.
- Married a wonderful man whom I love dearly
- Raised a fabulous son who I also love dearly.
- Homeschooled my son for 3 years
- Travelled to China, Italy, Europe, New Zealand, and the USA.
- Flying in a glider, a helicopter, a hot air balloon; piloting a Cessna.
- Learned the violin, then the guitar, the mandolin, the lute, and the tin whistle.
- Learned to sing opera and in choirs.
- Competed in Eisteddfodds and performing in school concerts and in professional stage musicals
- Acted in stage plays
- Competitive public speaking and debating
- Writing poetry and stories
- Composed music.
- Learned to bellydance
- Learned to paint in watercolours and acrylics.
- Learned basic pottery/pot-throwing
- Creating stained glass windows.
- Running successful small businesses

- Renovated 3 houses.
- Learned more about accounting software than I ever wanted to & trained hundreds of people how to use it.
- Multiple blackbelts in Aikido. Taught aikido students.
- Learned Brazilian jujitsu
- Learned to throw knives, and shoot longbow, recurve bow, and horsebow.
- Wrote 17 novels and 2 non fictions, plus multiple short stories. Edited 3 short story anthologies for my writers group.
- Taught multiple workshops to other writers

What are you waiting for? Get off the couch. Turn off the screen (unless you're in the middle of writing). Stop watching other people's lives and start living your own.

Have fun.

Discover other titles by Aiki Flinthart

at: **www.aikiflinthart.com**

Or

Blackbirds Sing (Historical fantasy)

The 80AD series (YA Adventure/Fantasy)
80AD Book 1: *The Jewel of Asgard*
80AD Book 2: *The Hammer of Thor*
80AD Book 3: *The Tekhen of Anuket*
80AD Book 4: *The Sudarshana*
80AD Book 5: *The Yu Dragon*

The Ruadhan Sidhe novels (YA Urban Fantasy)
Shadows Wake (#1)
Shadows Bane (#2)
Shadows Fate (#3)
Healing Heather (#4)(Romance)

The Kalima Chronicles (YA Sci/Fantasy)
IRON (#1)
FIRE (#2)
STEEL (#3)
A Future, Forged (Prequel)

Sold! (Contemporary Romance/Adventure)

Short Story Anthologies
Zookeeper's Tales of Interstellar Oddities
Return
Elemental
Rogues' Gallery

Non-Fiction – Author writing resources
Fight Like A *Girl* – Writing Fight Scenes for Female (and male) Characters
How to Get a Blackbelt in Writing

Connect with her on Facebook
https://www.facebook.com/aikiflinthartauthor
Twitter: @aikiflinthart
Instagram: Aikiflinthart

www.aikiflinthart.com

www.ingramcontent.com/pod-product-compliance
Lightning Source LLC
Chambersburg PA
CBHW030256010526
44107CB00053B/1735